Newcastle upon Tyne: the Guild Hall (foreground), the castle, the Moot Hall and the cathedral from Tyne Bridge.

Shire County Guide 30

NORTHUMBERLAND
and Newcastle upon Tyne

Priscilla Boniface and Peter Fowler

Shire Publications Ltd

CONTENTS

Copyright © 1989 by Priscilla Boniface and Peter Fowler. First published 1989. Shire County Guide 30. ISBN 0 85263 998 8.
All rights reserved. No part of this publication may be reproduced or transmitted in any form or by any means, electronic or mechanical, including photocopy, recording, or any information storage and retrieval system, without permission in writing from the publishers, Shire Publications Ltd, Cromwell House, Church Street, Princes Risborough, Aylesbury, Buckinghamshire HP17 9AJ, UK.

Printed in Great Britain by C. I. Thomas & Sons (Haverfordwest) Ltd, Press Buildings, Merlins Bridge, Haverfordwest, Dyfed SA61 1XF.

British Library Cataloguing in Publication Data: Boniface, Priscilla. Northumberland and Newcastle upon Tyne. — (Shire county guide; 30). 1. Tyne and Wear (Metropolitan County). Newcastle upon Tyne — Visitors' guides. 2. Northumberland — Visitors' guides. I. Title. II Fowler, Peter 1942 —. 914.28' 7604858. ISBN 0-85263-998-8.

ACKNOWLEDGEMENTS
All the photographs, printed by Monochrome in the St Thomas Street Workshops, Newcastle upon Tyne, are by the authors except for those on pages 40 (left) by Mick Sharp of Caernarfon and pages 1, 3, 5, 17, 23, 27, 28, 29, 30, 31, 33, 35, 36, 37, 40 (right), 43 (right), 44, 46, 52, 53, 60 by Cadbury Lamb. The maps were drawn by D. R. Darton.

Cover: *Warkworth Castle.*

BELOW: *Hines' Cottages, Old Mousen.*

2

Alnwick Castle across the Aln.

1
County and city

Northumberland is promoted by the tourist industry as 'England's undiscovered county' and Newcastle is hardly at the top of every tourist's list. The relative remoteness, psychologically as well as geographically, of the county and city from much of the rest of England is what makes the area such an attractive place in which to live and so enjoyable a place for its discerning, often regular, visitors.

They have discovered for themselves what may well appear to be nothing more than the truism that the present nature of the region is very much a product of its history. What they will have come to appreciate is the combination of history and present-day culture, of provincial capital and predominantly rural region, of natural beauty and industrial detritus, with people forever friendly, locally patriotic to the extent of chauvinism, and undoubtedly 'canny'.

The key to the distinctiveness of both Northumberland and Newcastle is their position on a frontier. Northumberland contains England's northernmost lands; at times they were Scotland's southernmost. Newcastle is England's northernmost city, crucial to the front line. Such language smacks of military affairs, and in this far English north this is unavoidable and indeed appropriate. To the north of it were hostile peoples, an alien state even, circumstances which have stamped so

much on the landscape and history, indeed on the whole character, of county and city. Such a state of affairs was long-lived too: long after the union of Scottish and English crowns in 1603 and the formal political union with Scotland in 1707, long after the rest of England had settled down in relatively civil order, frontier troubles continued.

Nor is the border framework of life in Northumberland just a characteristic of medieval and later times. A thousand years earlier, another frontier, also facing north, was drawn and defended. That Hadrian's Wall was an imperial frontier, not just a national or provincial one, emphasises the marginal nature of this area.

Nevertheless, Northumbria emerged in the post-Roman period as the first Anglo-Saxon kingdom with some claim to supremacy over others, a development of considerable significance for the future England. That this Anglian kingdom lay in the frontier zone between two different and increasingly competitive versions of Christian expression also made it the stage, centred on Lindisfarne, for missionary zeal, confrontation and compromise crucial for the development of the church in England. And it was in the emergent institutionalised church that there occurred either side of AD 700 that flowering of artistic and scholastic achievement which led to 'the Golden Age of Northumbria', a tag associated above all with the Lindisfarne Gospels and the Venerable Bede, the first great English historian.

The world epitomised by Bede disappeared with the internal disintegration of the Northumbrian kingdom and external attacks by the Vikings from the late eighth century onwards. Its Christian centres suffered in what became a long travail, epitomised by the travels of the relics of another great Northumbrian man of the church, St Cuthbert. Perhaps, however, the most lasting effect on England north of York was perpetrated by the Normans after 1066. The area of the future county of Northumberland was carved up among new estate holders and planted with castles in alien hands, probably as much to subdue the locals as to keep the Scots at bay.

It was then that the building of the new castle at the lowest crossing point from (or to) the north bank of the river Tyne provided the core for the settlement that was to grow, eventually, to become the city of Newcastle upon Tyne. The Norman castle stood, for tactical reasons, on the same site as the Roman fort. During the twelfth and thirteenth centuries an urban settlement was growing, as a port with a developing quayside pushing out over the muddy shore, and as a town of considerable area with an impressive wall fitted with defensive gates. One, the Westgate, was at a point where the line of the city wall crossed Hadrian's Wall, a position through which still passes the city's main exit to the west, the A6115/69 to Carlisle.

By 1300 Newcastle was on the way to becoming one of the more important English provincial capitals, vying nationally with Norwich and Bristol. In effect it also became the county town of Northumberland, at least in economic terms. An interesting relationship compound of common interest and mutual suspicion survived the centuries but by the mid eighteenth century county and city were changing. In some respects they were to go separate ways; in others, though the nature of their relationship changed, their ties became closer.

Along both banks of the Tyne industrialisation developed on a scale and at a speed not previously experienced. The area was in the front line of technological development, ultimately of worldwide significance. The so-called industrial revolution was happening elsewhere too but in those decades Tyneside contributed enormously to a great surge in inventiveness and productivity. In the process, Newcastle changed from a medieval border town to first an urban mess and then a would-be grandiose, modern regional capital.

It became the centre of a great industrial conurbation. By the time of Clayton, Grainger and Dobson in the 1830s the distinction between the city and its industrial context on the one hand and the county on the other was clearly marked. Newcastle was not just a larger Alnwick. Its reputation was as *the* exporting harbour for coal but the trade was only capable of such remarkable growth in the nineteenth century because the coal-mining industry expanded enormously. Spurred by increased demand, production increased as an

Rus in urbe: Tyneside allotment at show time.

4

Limekilns in the care of the National Trust at Beadnell.

improving technology for drilling, draining and hauling was applied. Tyneside's other well known strength was in shipbuilding; indeed it became one of Britain's great shipbuilding areas. In addition, there was heavy engineering, an early and successful chemical industry, a glass industry, a mass-production pottery industry and, later in the nineteenth century, a great armaments industry.

The industrial zone spread out of its narrow confines in the lower Tyne valley, although it was always small in relation to the rest of the county. Essentially it consisted of a narrow rectangular strip, west-east along the Tyne for some 15 miles (24 km) and south-north for slightly further up the coast but not extending inland west of the Great North Road. Apart from lead mining on the North Pennines and pockets of extractive industry elsewhere, the rest of the county was, and remains, beautifully unspoilt.

The later eighteenth and nineteenth centuries, then, produced a visually clear separation between Newcastle at the centre of the industrialised conurbation and the quietly rural aspect of the other nine-tenths of the county. However, despite appearances, the relationship between county and city became very close. Money generated on Tyneside by industry and commerce moved into the county and made a palpable impact in producing the rural landscape we see today.

Fishing boats returning to Lindisfarne harbour past the navigation obelisks.

2
The countryside

England does not end with Newcastle; neither is the Roman Wall the border with Scotland. Northumberland fills the area north and north-west of Newcastle to the border with Scotland. Its south-eastern corner was transferred in 1974 into the Metropolitan County of Tyne and Wear, an arrangement ignored in this book.

It is 60 miles (96 km) from Newcastle to Berwick-upon-Tweed and there are 3½ more miles (5.5 km) of England and Northumberland beyond that. From Tynemouth Priory on the coast to Gilsland on the border with Cumbria to the west is 46 miles (74 km), and south of the Tyne is an area some 15 by 35 miles (24 by 56 km). In all, Northumberland covers about 2000 square miles (5200 sq km), nearly all of it countryside.

Geologically and topographically the county is quite complex but essentially it is of four zones. In the south-west, south of the river South Tyne and butting on to both County Durham and Cumbria, are the North Pennines. This area, underlain by Carboniferous limestone and millstone grit, has predominantly acid, peaty soils. It is characterised by drystone walls, the evidence of former lead mining and, now, by sweeps of wild moorland with hill farming up to well over a thousand feet (300 metres) above sea level. Part of the North Pennine Area of Outstanding Natural Beauty, it is also a watershed area draining into the Durham dales eastwards, the Irish Sea westwards and into the Tyne basin to the north.

Though broken by the Tyne Gap, the high land continues northwards from the North Pennines as largely sheep-grazed, heather-covered moorland. Its climax is the Cheviot massif spanning the Anglo-Scots border. At its highest 2676 feet (816 metres) above sea level, Cheviot itself is a long-defunct volcano, now capped by a rather messy peat bog. The Cheviot Hills are characterised by grass cover, ideal for thousands of sheep but probably as little lived in by man now as at any time in the last five thousand years.

Virtually the whole of the high land characterising this second zone is within the Northumberland National Park. The Army occupies part of it on the Otterburn Ranges. The other major land use is forestry. The Forestry Commission's Kielder Forest blankets in softwoods a huge area from Redesdale, across the headwaters of the North Tyne, dammed in the great Kielder Reservoir, to within sight of Hadrian's Wall.

The third zone can be designated as the mid Northumberland plain. Basically it consists of a relatively low-lying plateau on Carboniferous limestone with projections of fell sandstones and cementstones. Much of it is overlain with boulder clay and loams which stretch from the Tyne to the Tweed between the hills on the west and the coast to the east. Gently rolling countryside supports mixed farming, served by most of the county's main towns, and carrying the main through road and rail routes. At its south-east corner is the industrial strip; otherwise, it is a 'civilised' landscape of estates, country houses, villages and hamlets, enclosed fields and amenity woodland.

Northumberland is scenically fortunate in also containing a wonderful coastline, here the fourth zone. Some 50 miles (80 km) of almost unspoilt, unbroken sandy beach, dunes and cliffs stretch north from Druridge Bay to Marshall Meadows Bay some 3 miles (5 km) north of Berwick. Much of it is designated Heritage Coast and also an Area of Outstanding Natural Beauty; furthermore, considerable lengths, and the Farne Islands, are owned by the National Trust.

While the broad sweeps of golden sand and the wind-blown marram of the dunes provide the scenic quality, the zone is of great scientific and historical importance too. Coquet Island, off Amble, is owned by the Royal Society for the Protection of Birds and human visitors are not allowed. Part of Holy Island and much of the adjacent intertidal flats are within a large National Nature Reserve protecting birds and the coastal ecology; the National Trust and English Heritage afford protection to the architecturally significant buildings of a place enmeshed in religiosity and military history. Indeed, from Tynemouth to Berwick is a whole series of castles and other defensive structures, notably lonely Dunstanburgh Castle, the romantically upstanding Bamburgh Castle and Berwick's superb sixteenth-century defences.

Except for the mouth of the river Wansbeck, all the major estuaries — of the Tyne (North Shields), Blyth (Blyth), Coquet (Amble), Aln (Alnmouth) and Tweed (Tweedmouth/Berwick) — have been fashioned into harbours. With less obvious natural advantages and with much use of sturdy walls, harbours were also built at Cullercoats, Seaton Sluice, Craster, Beadnell, Seahouses and Lindisfarne. Some of these places are still fishing villages, and fishing, now along with an increase in leisure boating, is also carried out from various 'havens', as at Low Newton, or simply from the beach, as at Boulmer. A marina has been opened at Amble.

Northumberland possesses another marked characteristic in its landscape: its river valleys. With two main exceptions, the upper reaches of the river South Tyne and the river Till, all the main rivers run from west to east, off the high ground, through the middle plain and out through the coastal zone. Together they provide some of Northumberland's most varied and attractive countryside: the moorland burns, sometimes babbling through patches of ancient woodland; the narrow, steep-sided, flat-bottomed valleys of Cheviot country; the thickly wooded valleys of the lower reaches of the rivers Blyth, Wansbeck and Coquet; the rich agricultural lands of the North Tyne around Chollerford and of the Tweed basin. Fresh water tends to reach the North Sea rather sluggishly so there are many examples of ponding up just behind the sand-dunes. This adds to the range of habitats which make Northumberland extremely attractive to birds — and therefore to birdwatchers.

Northumberland seems made for moving around in. Its very emptiness invites not so much mass tourism but the walker, the cyclist, the horse-rider and the car-borne explorer. Its sporting attractions include the traditional ones of hunting, shooting, fishing and golf as well as more fashionable ones like hanggliding, sailing, surfing and, unfortunately, microlight flying. The Pennine Way winds through the western parts of the county, part of it following some of the best stretches of the Roman Wall. The county is also laced with a network of signposted rights of way and, in general, access to the countryside and the coast is not difficult.

Wooded valley and burn north of Blanchland.

CHAPTER 2

The weather is not as bad as many people think it is, though there is usually a wind and, largely as a result, air temperatures seldom become hot. There are many days with long hours of sunshine, but winter, which can be extreme, tends to continue into April and even May, and autumn to start in August. The best months for visiting are May and June, and September can produce lovely Indian summers.

Allenbanks, near Haydon Bridge (OS 86/87: NY 799630). National Trust.

A pretty and secluded place close to the junction of the rivers Allen and Tyne, Allenbanks was originally planted as a Georgian landscape for nearby Ridley Hall. The property contains a variety of terrain covering nearly 200 acres (80 ha), with walks along the river Allen, woodlands, a tarn and, from the hilltop above the east bank of the river, a good view to Hadrian's Wall. The wildlife includes red squirrels and roe deer, with wildfowl on the tarn.

Bedlington Country Park, Humford Mill, Church Lane, Bedlington NE22 5RT. Telephone: 0670 829550.

Bedlington Country Park has an informa-

The Pennine Way descending to Redesdale through Kielder Forest.

tion centre, horse-riding and nature trails and picnic areas.

Bolam Lake Country Park, Bolam, near Belsay. Telephone: 066181 234 or 0434 605555.

Administered by Northumberland County Council, this is one of the most pleasant places to visit within easy driving distance of Newcastle. The country park, a lake set in woodland, formed part of the Bolam Hall estate and was landscaped by the local architect John Dobson in 1818. The park is provided with a car park and special picnic places and there are various themed trails. Bolam was once a town with a castle and two hundred houses round a green; the church is part Anglo-Saxon (see chapter 5).

Coquet Island, Amble. Royal Society for the Protection of Birds. Information from Amble tourist information centre: telephone: 0665 712313.

Coquet Island, a mile off shore, is a reserve for thousands of puffins, terns and eider ducks, and boat trips around the island are organised by the RSPB from the harbour at Amble.

Derwent Reservoir, west of Consett. Information: telephone Northumberland County Council, 0670 514343.

The reservoir straddles the boundary of Northumberland and County Durham. On the Northumbrian side, at the eastern end below Minsteracres, is the delightful and low-key Millshield picnic site at a point alongside the reservoir where it curves into an inlet. The location is a favourite with fishermen. A little further west along the attractive north shore road is a sailing club, and beyond that is a nature reserve. There are good views to the surrounding Pennine hills.

Farne Islands. Telephone: 0665 720424. National Trust. Information from the National Trust Information Centre, 16 Main Street, Seahouses.

The group of Farne Islands are outcrops of the Whin Sill. In good weather boat trips from Seahouses round the islands may allow landing on either or both of Inner Farne and Staple Island.

The islands are the summer home and nesting ground of a variety of seabirds and the location of a large colony of grey seals. The seasonal birdlife includes kittiwakes, puffins, guillemots, fulmars, terns and eider ducks. On these islands, birds and animals take priority and their welfare is of the prime importance. Consequently there is only limited public access to some islands, and it is not possible for the public to land at all on most of them.

On the Inner Farne, which is open to the

Off Millshield shore, Derwent Reservoir.

public, St Cuthbert died in AD 687, and he is commemorated by a fourteenth-century chapel, which was restored in 1845. Alongside, in the former chapel of St Mary, is a small exhibition about the islands. The tower house nearby was built in the later medieval period by Prior Castell. A short walk over ridge and furrow, presumably the monastic arable field, leads to the lighthouse, built in 1809. There was a long association between the lightkeeping family of the heroine Grace Darling and the islands. Grace's grandfather began the tradition when he assumed responsibility for looking after the new beacon on Staple Island. There are remains of a beacon on Brownsman Island. Grace was living at the lighthouse on Longstone Island when she and her father set out in 1838 on their epic mission of rescue. On Staple Island and Inner Farne there are nature trails. The more fertile islands are rich in flora, including the white-flowered sea campion.

Hareshaw Linn, Hareshaw Dene, Bellingham. Telephone: 067074 660. Northumberland National Park.

This beautiful waterfall at the head of the wooded valley of the Hareshaw Burn is associated with other small waterfalls along the way up the gorge, with semi-natural woodland flora. The remains of nineteenth-century ironworks can be seen at the start of the walk and so too in places along the valley can the old railway line used for transporting coal and iron.

Kielder Water and Forest

A road runs along the south shore of the lake but on the north shore there are only cycling, horse-riding and walking trails through a 'wilderness' district. Kielder is a large country leisure area, reminiscent of an American national park.

Bakethin Reservoir. This area is especially devoted to the conservation of wildlife and there is only restricted visitor access. Nearby is the track of the old North Tyne Railway.

Kielder Castle Visitor Centre. Telephone: 0660 20242. Forestry Commission. In a Gothick shooting box built for the Duke of Northumberland in 1775 are an exhibition on the forest and a cafe. Observation hides to see wildlife are nearby. Close to the castle is the starting point for a tolled 12 mile (19 km) scenic forest drive through to Redesdale, where the A68 is joined not far from Catcleugh Reservoir.

Kielder Water Visitor Centre, Tower Knowe, Yarrow Moor, Bellingham, Hexham NE48 1BX. Telephone: 0660 40398. Northumberland National Park and Northumbrian Water. The facilities include a film show and exhibition, a shop and a cafe. In summer a ferry goes to various points round the lake.

Leaplish Waterside Park. Provision is made for a variety of water sports such as sailing, swimming and windsurfing. Other facilities include log cabins and a caravan and camp site. At Matthews Linn boats may be hired and angling permits obtained. The road up the Lewis Burn leads to a picnic site.

Kilham Farm Walk, Kilham. Off B6351 between Kirknewton and Town Yetholm, take the minor road south through Kilham village to the marked starting point.

Leaflets are available from the end of May to September for this self-guided walk of about 4 miles (6 km) over private land on the Kilham

Crowded cliffs on the Farne Islands.

Estate in the northern Cheviots.

Once Brewed Information Centre, Military Road, Bardon Mill, Hexham NE47 7AN. Telephone: 04984 396.

Conveniently situated beside B6318 in the centre of Hadrian's Wall country near Steel Rigg car park and between Housesteads and Carvoran, this national park facility includes information and material on Hadrian's Wall as well as toilets, a car park and the usual tourist information.

Plessey Woods Country Park, Shields Road, Hartford. Telephone: 0670 824793.

Beyond the golf course, on the south-western outskirts of Bedlington, is Plessey Woods Country Park, which extends along the banks of the river Blyth and encompasses Plessey Mill. The park has a small camp site and a visitor centre. There are various special trails.

Rothley Crags, Rothley, near Cambo.

Formerly part of the Wallington estate, the Crags were a sightseeing venue for Sir Walter Calverly Blackett and his Wallington guests in the eighteenth century: they both form a landmark and provide sweeping views to the west and south. A small, late prehistoric

hillfort occupies the ground above the precipitous western rock face; the whole area was later a deer park and, more recently, an alarm beacon inside the hillfort warned of approaching Scottish raiders. Nearby Rothley Lake was designed by 'Capability' Brown. Immediately visible from the road are two eyecatchers: one, Rothley Castle, built as a folly to the design of Daniel Garrett in the 1740s, is now in a sad state of disrepair and dangerously close to collapse; the other, Codger's Fort (National Trust), a short distance to the north and looking even more like a sham castle, was built in 1769.

Simonside Forest Walks, 2 miles south west of Rothbury. Car park and leaflets at OS 87: NZ 037997, off minor road between B6340 and Great Tosson.

A choice of waymarked walks, varying from ½-2½ hours or even longer, leads up through Forestry Commission plantations on to wild and craggy moorland with uninterrupted views to Cheviot, the coast and the south.

St Mary's Island, Whitley Bay. Telephone: 091 2520853.

Cut off from the mainland at high tide, the former Trinity House lighthouse was built in 1896-8 as a replacement for the lighthouse on the promontory close to Tynemouth Priory, by then 'enveloped in smoke from the Tyne'. The St Mary's lighthouse was de-commissioned in 1984 and is now open to the public, providing spectacular coastal views from the top. There is a birdwatching hide, and in the former lightkeeper's house is a visitor centre with an exhibition on the history and wildlife of this area. In 1855 a croft was built on the island for salmon fishermen; it became a pub, the Square and Compass, and, little altered and with great atmosphere, it is now a cafe. The flora and fauna, especially the marine life in the rock pools, make St Mary's and its environs a very interesting place.

Tyne Riverside Country Park, Station Road, Prudhoe. Telephone: 0661 34135.

From Low Prudhoe Visitor Centre, the park extends eastwards to Newburn through Wylam and includes areas on both sides of the Tyne in its designated area. A variety of habitats within the park includes calcareous grassland, scrubland, broad-leaved and coniferous woodland and pasture, as well as riverside. There are picnic sites at Low Prudhoe, Hagg Bank, Wylam and Newburn.

St Mary's Island at low water.

Moorland landscape, Allendale.

3
Sites of archaeological interest

Northumberland contains one of the best arrays of upstanding archaeological sites in any English county. Its field archaeology is remarkable for its excellent quality in terms of preservation, range, variety and detail, and for its quantity. On the sides of one small valley, that of the river Breamish, for example, are more visible, visitable prehistoric and Romano-British settlements than there now are in the whole of East Anglia.

So much of the county is grassland and moorland, basically undisturbed for the last two or even four thousand years, that settlements by the hundred have survived, often associated with parts of their contemporary landscapes in the form of field systems, cairnfields and burial mounds. Nor does this apply only to prehistoric remains. The Hadrian's Wall area is a World Heritage Site (see chapter 4); military and civil remains of the Roman period are also liberally scattered across the landscape elsewhere. Fine examples of deserted medieval settlements survive. Furthermore, in certain areas, notably Allendale and Redesdale, early industry developed and its remains now provide another archaeological layer to the existing landscape.

The following list includes but a fraction of what exists in Northumberland. It contains merely a selection of the sites that are marked on the Ordnance Survey 1:50,000 maps, and they show only a small percentage of the twenty thousand or more sites so far recorded in the county. Nevertheless, the best advice is to acquire the relevant sheets of the OS 1:50,000 maps (the Landranger series). Sheets 74 and 75 are particularly rewarding and sheet 80 is very useful too. Better still, buy the appropriate 1:25,000 sheets (OS Pathfinder series), which show the footpaths and the archaeology more fully. But outsiders keen to venture into the hills on foot must be warned: never underestimate the Northumbrian weather.

Bellshiel Law, Rochester (OS 80: NT 813014). East of the minor road through Redesdale army camp off A68, its east end marked by a plantation.

This rare example in Northumberland of a well preserved long cairn probably dates from the later third millennium BC. 113 metres (370 feet) long and just over 1 metre (3 feet 3 inches) high, its mound of boulders and stones was retained by a drystone kerb. A grave lay in the eastern end. A group of round cairns lies about 100 metres (110 yards) south-east.

Brough Law, Ingram (OS 81: NT 998164). Walk up from the road in the Breamish valley.

This small stone-built fort 290 metres (950 feet) above sea-level commands superb views up, down and across the valley in a landscape dotted with prehistoric sites. The ramparts are dated by carbon-14 assay to c.300 BC. Traces of timber and stone round buildings exist inside, the latter probably of Roman date.

Chew Green Roman camps (OS 80: NT 787085). The site can be reached only on foot, from the west along the Pennine Way, from the south along Dere Street, and from the east along the military track (no unauthorised vehicles) continuing the minor road from the upper reaches of Upper Coquetdale.

The walks through some of the wildest country in the Borders are rewarded by one of the great earthwork complexes of Roman Britain, its preservation understandably due to its remote position. Four rectilinear Roman works are visible, all superimposed and inter-meshed: an Agricolan marching camp of AD c.80, the most extensive of the visible camps and large enough to take a legion; a mid second-century temporary camp mainly to the north but overlapping the first camp's north side; a labour camp entirely within the first camp; and, on top of the first camp's east side, a permanent fortlet with three ditches, except on its south where there are two conjoined annexes interpreted as wagon parks.

Dod Hill, Ilderton (OS 75: NT 987207).

A long cairn, one of the very few examples in Northumberland of a neolithic burial mound, is 24 metres (79 feet) long and 1.5 metres (5 feet) high, 325 metres (1066 feet) above sea level on the southern slopes of the hill.

Dod Law, Doddington (OS 75: around NU 005317). On Doddington Moor south-east of the village, approached on foot by several marked footpaths or up the road to the golf club (private parking only).

This is an area to explore on foot rather than suitable for a quick visit. A small but promin-ent late prehistoric hillfort overlooks the Mil-field basin below and to the west, with Cheviot forming an impressive western skyline. Ex-cavations have demonstrated the late prehis-toric structural succession of the ramparts, apparently continuing into the Roman period, when the site was also occupied. Its interior contains the clearly visible walls of round buildings; entrances are to the south-east and north-west. Immediately north of the site are some of the best examples in the county of prehistoric rock art of c.2000 BC and later, pecked into the surface of sandstones at or just above ground level; and many other examples are scattered over the moor, for example at NU 011312, 004318, 005317.

Duddo stone circle (OS 75: NT 931437). Approachable only on foot; walk north along a track from the minor road going west out of Duddo.

The five standing stones, about 2 metres (6½ feet) high, are clearly visible on the skyline of a low knoll. Originally there were more, forming a circle some 10 metres (33 feet) in diameter c.2000 BC.

Five Barrows, Holystone (OS 81: NT 953020). Footpath to south from village.

Nine cairns up to 18 metres (59 feet) in diameter and 1 metre (3¼ feet) high make up this cemetery which contained both inhuma-tions and cremations during its use in the second millennium BC.

Fredden Hill cairnfield, near Wooler (OS 75: NT 950270). East of a plantation on the north side of the private road leading to Common-burn House.

This is a typical example of what is almost certainly the commonest, and least well known, type of prehistoric site on North-umberland's uplands, a cairnfield. More than a hundred small mounds here are the result of clearing the ground for prehistoric agriculture, probably in the second millennium BC.

Greave's Ash settlements, Ingram (OS 81: NT 965164). Park on roadside before Hartside Farm and walk west towards Linhope but bearing north towards a plantation on the hillside. The site is behind it over the brow of the hill.

This is a well preserved double-ramparted settlement of the last centuries BC, also occupied in the early centuries AD when the settlement spread outside to the east for some 100 metres (330 feet). A similar settlement with round stone-footed buildings lies a furth-er 100 metres east; and south of it is another, later settlement with long rectangular building foundations visible.

Harehaugh camp, Holystone (OS 81: NY 969998). Immediately south of the minor road from Holystone to Swindon, follow a path up to the hilltop.

Above the junction of two streams, this small (1.3 ha or 3¼ acres) enclosed site is typical of many so-called 'hillforts' in North-umberland. Its multiple banks and ditches demonstrate at least two phases of construc-tion. Two entrances exist on its west; a possible third exists on the north-east.

Hartside, Ingram (OS 81: NT 985176). Walk north up to the site from the road up the Ingram valley.

This is a well preserved example of a deserted medieval settlement high in what is now virtually uninhabited country but which was formerly more fully settled, despite its proximity to the Scottish border.

Haystack Hill, Ingram (OS 81: NU 005150). Walk south-west up the footpath from the west end of Ingram village.

The grid reference is to the Romano-British settlements, which are embedded in a complex of earthworks, and these extend all along the southeast-facing slopes from Ewe Hill down Middledean Burn. Indeed, the field systems also spread further up the slope east of the burn and are best seen from the Haystack Hill side. Among the many features in the area are a late prehistoric palisaded settlement containing much later rectangular houses (NU 011158) and a small but impressive hillfort, its ramparts of at least two phases, perched above a steep drop into Middledean (NU 004146).

Hethpool stone circle, College Valley (OS 74: NT 892278). West of the bridlepath which runs on from the minor road from Westnewton to Hethpool.

Eight stones about 2 metres (6½ feet) high indicate a former circle some 60 metres (200 feet) in diameter. Three other stones, perhaps part of that circle, occur to the north-east, the most southerly one ring-marked.

High Knowes, Alnham (OS 81: NT 971125). Take the minor road north-west out of the village and then walk up to the top of the hill on the right about 2½ miles out.

Two palisaded enclosures of the mid first millennium BC are marvellously preserved in the grass with the detail of their entrances and hut stances clearly visible. The round stone footings in the lower enclosure are of the Roman period. A cairnfield exists either side of the road; some of its cairns contained prehistoric burials.

Knock Hill, Ingram (OS 81: NT 995173).

Three round burial cairns of the second millennium BC, typical of many of the hundreds of such mounds in the county in that they occupy a prominent position on a hilltop, have been dug into by antiquarians and have been robbed of some of their stones. They form part of the spread of prehistoric burial mounds and settlements along the north side of the Breamish valley.

Lordenshaws, Hesleyhurst (OS 81: NZ 055993). A footpath from a metalled track north of B6342 leads to the hillfort.

The hillfort is one of the more impressive small, late prehistoric defended sites in the county, partly because of its siting on a spur, partly because of its multi-ramparted complexity and good preservation. The circular stone

foundations inside are of the Roman period; they also overlie the south-eastern defences. The site is in an area of considerable archaeological interest, containing a cairnfield to the north-east and two groups of decorated stones about 300 metres (330 yards) to the south-west. The ruinous wall west of the hillfort is of a medieval deer park.

Old Bewick hillfort (OS 75: NU 075216). Up a steep path east out of the village.

Well worth the climb for the view alone, the unusual site on the hilltop consists of two conjoined embanked enclosures of the last centuries BC. To their south-east is a group of rocks with cup-and-ring marks.

Old Yeavering (OS 75: NT 926305). On the north side of B6351.

This site is of great importance in the history of England and of archaeology itself. Unfortunately, nothing is now visible except for a modern monument beside the road recording that here, beside the river Glen, was almost certainly the site of the royal palace of King Edwin visited in AD 627 by the missionary Paulinus, bringing 'Roman' Christianity to the pagan Anglo-Saxon kingdom of Northumbria.

Roughting Linn, Doddington (OS 75: NT 984367). On the west side of the minor road between A697 and B6525.

A slab of sandstone is covered in spectacular fashion by a variety of motifs laboriously pecked out c.2000 BC and probably later. Its setting is just outside and east of the multiple ramparts of an unusual, low-lying prehistoric enclosure near the junction of two streams in attractive woodland.

Welton, Ovingham (OS 87: NY 063676). Turn south off B6318 at Whittingdean reservoirs for 500 yards. No public right of access but view from road.

The pele tower sticking up from the cluster of farm buildings at the hall is part of a substantial medieval building. Between the hall, a private farmhouse, and Welton Farm 1 km (⅝ mile) to the west are two fields full of excellently preserved earthworks representing a formerly large village. The remains are the foundations of some fifty buildings standing in their closes arranged along a central hollow-way, once the village street.

Wooler hillfort (OS 75: NT 984274). A bridle-path leads south-west out of the town.

One of the larger hillforts around the fringes of Cheviot, this encloses 1.8 ha (4½ acres) of a promontory overlooking Wooler and the Milfield basin. The earthworks are complex, with entrances to north and south and internal divisions.

Yeavering Bell hillfort (OS 75: NT 928293). Walk from Wooler across the waymarked moorland paths or climb the footpath up the steep northern slope from the farm at Old Yeavering off B6351.

The views from the top across the Borders, the Milfield basin and, immediately below, the royal Anglo-Saxon site at Old Yeavering, are superb. The largest hillfort in Northumberland, its 5.3 ha (13 acres) are enclosed by a single stone rampart which embraces both knolls of the hilltop; a palisade trench encircles the eastern knoll. Platforms for well over a hundred round buildings are clearly visible in the turf over the interior.

4
Hadrian's Wall

Hadrian's Wall is rightly regarded as one of the great archaeological monuments of the world — it was accorded the status of a World Heritage Site in 1987 — and as a staggering achievement of the Romans in Britain. Indeed, it has been described as 'perhaps the largest and most remarkable building programme ever undertaken in these islands at any time'. Certainly, in terms of the manual labour involved, it is on a par with the building of a main-line railway in the mid nineteenth century.

It did not just happen, however, in a void or on a whim. As the Roman army pushed north in the second half of the first century AD, a frontier was established along the Tyne and Irthing valleys between a fort just west of the present village of Corbridge and another one across the river north of present-day Carlisle. This frontier apparently consisted of forts along a road, the Stanegate. They were basic to the original plan for the new frontier ordered by Hadrian in the 120s AD. The main feature was to be a stone wall from Newcastle to the river Irthing, extended westward to the Solway Firth in turf, with milecastles at regular intervals subdivided into three lengths by two stone turrets. Both sorts of 'interval towers' were continued down the Cumbrian coast to Maryport, adding 26 miles to the 73 miles (80 Roman miles, 117 km) from Wallsend on Tyne to Bowness-on-Solway.

This plan was changed during construction. First, forts were added to the Wall and then the rear of the military zone was sealed off with the vallum. This is perhaps the least appreciated and most enigmatic of the frontier elements. Essentially it consists of a central ditch between turf-built banks; it ran from Tyne to Solway and is probably best regarded as the Roman equivalent of a rolled barbed-wire barricade. No one found on the wrong

The Wall's uncompleted ditch cutting through rock at Limestone Corner, Teppermore Hill.

side of it, that is between it and the Wall, could claim that they had not noticed it.

In the same military zone was a military road (the Military Way, not to be confused with General Wade's Military Road of the mid eighteenth century which ran between Newcastle and Carlisle and is now followed in its turn by the B6318). The Romans' road was built to service the Wall laterally, while supplies also entered up the Tyne from the storage depot at South Shields and along the main roads from the south, across the *Pons Aelius* at Newcastle, and through Corbridge, Carvoran and Carlisle.

When visiting the Wall area, then, it is important not just to look at the Wall itself but to see it as part of a complex frontier zone consisting of several elements. Furthermore, the frontier acquired its own history during the three centuries or so of its Roman existence; and it remained a frontier zone into the eighteenth century. The Roman Wall was by no means intended as an impenetrable barrier, nor did it prove permanent: it was, for example, replaced by the Antonine Wall in Scotland as Rome's north-western frontier for a short period soon after it was built, and then it was recommissioned; and it is generally agreed that, far from being unbreachable, one of its main purposes was to control, not stop, north-south traffic.

Another function was almost certainly to divide, not exclude, native communities, in particular to put a bar between the Brigantes to the south and the Selgovae to the north. The Wall itself was not a fighting platform similar to the walls of medieval castles. Rather it was a barrier with lookout posts behind which troops could be assembled out of sight to sally forth unexpectedly from various gates when the need arose.

Visitors to the area will find the Wall zone easy of access by car but difficult for the casual walker. Buses from Newcastle now make special Wall trips; otherwise, take the Carlisle train and walk, take a taxi or hope for the occasional bus, from Corbridge, Hexham, Haydon Bridge, Bardon Mill, Haltwhistle or Greenhead.

Many of the roads in the area, especially the B6318, are not suitable for the amount and speed of modern traffic and can be highly dangerous, especially for walkers. Be careful: do not let your search for the past curtail your future.

The entries are arranged east to west. Milecastles and turrets are numbered likewise, the latter designated a and b following the number of the milecastle to their east.

Wallsend: fort (*Segedunum*) and heritage centre (OS 88: NZ 301661).

The fort was completely excavated in the 1970s. Its outline is now laid out in a densely built-up area on an open site dramatically overshadowed by the shipbuilding yard between it and the river Tyne. Remains of the headquarters building are consolidated in position. The fort is at the east end of the Wall, was built under Hadrian and went through many structural changes during its use, which lasted to the end of the fourth century AD. The Wall itself takes off west-southwest from immediately south of the west gate and, a short distance to the west, its foundations are being excavated with a view to consolidation and display. The Heritage Centre (see chapter 8) is just outside the north-east corner of the fort and displays some of the material and information from the excavations.

Newcastle: fort (*Pons Aelius*) (OS 88: NZ 250638).

None of the original structure is now visible. The outlines of part of the fort discovered in excavation, however, are picked out in stones at pavement level around the Norman keep and beneath the railway viaduct in a presentation which requires some imagination to appreciate the three major different uses of this key site, the core of Newcastle, overlooking the lowest bridgeable point on the river Tyne. The Museum of Antiquities, the major Wall museum (see chapter 8), containing many of the objects associated with it and a scale model of the whole Wall, is immediately within the university precinct just off Haymarket (from which it is signposted).

Benwell: vallum crossing and temple (OS 88: NZ 215646).

Two small glimpses of the complexities of the Wall, preserved after excavation and displayed in a suburban area, the sites are signposted to the south off the main west road (A69) out of Newcastle. A fort (*Condercum*) lies under the A69 and the vallum bends southwards to go round it. The visible causeway carried the road out of the fort's south gateway across the vallum ditch; on it was a stone portal (model in the Museum of Antiquities, Newcastle).

The temple lies round the houses about 270 yards (250 metres) west. It was to a local god, Antenociticus, whose bust, with the originals of two altars dedicated to him, is also in the Museum of Antiquities. The head was probably part of a statue which stood in the apse behind the two altars (copies on site).

Denton Hall: Wall and turret (OS 88: NZ 196657).

Several fragments of the Wall are visible on the south side of the A69, itself following the mid eighteenth-century Military Road overlying the ditch of the Wall, as it leaves

Corbridge: the site of the fountain and the modern museum.

Newcastle. Not to be missed is the pathetic mortared little heap of stones in the forecourt of the petrol station at Silver Lonnen round-about; a little further west, and rather more prominent, one of the preserved lengths of Wall incorporates Denton Hall turret (7b). Excavations near here in 1988, where the western bypass cuts through the line of the Roman frontier works, showed how unsoph-isticated were the construction methods on what may well have been a length of Wall built in the first months of the project. The vallum ditch, however, was impressively cut 2 metres (6½ feet) deep through solid rock.

Heddon-on-the-Wall (OS 88: NZ 137669).

Again on the south side of the Military Way, here now the B6528 (which has been super-seded by the modern A69), the Wall is represented by the longest visible stretch of 3 metres (10 feet) wide ('broad') foundations. The kiln is post-medieval.

Corbridge: Roman town and museum (OS 87: NY 983647). English Heritage.

This site is not on the line of Hadrian's Wall but it was crucial to the changing fortunes of the Roman frontier zone over four centuries. Its importance derives in large part from its position at a crossing of the river Tyne — it lay above the north end of a bridge — and at the junction of the main road to the north, Dere Street, and the main east-west road, Stane-gate.

Its own functions changed too: it was a fort in the 80s AD, became a storage and supply base in the later second century and developed into a considerable civil settlement. It is important to appreciate, when looking at the exposed remains, that they display only the military core of a much larger site which is known to exist under the grass and arable fields beyond the fences of the preserved monument. The Roman settlement stretched east, for example, much nearer to the site of the present village of Corbridge than appears to be the case; and the early fort lies across the Cor Burn, about 1 km (⅝ mile) north-west and cut by the A69, with its bath-house to its south on the north bank of the Redhouse Burn.

On the site itself, the granaries are arguably the most impressive in Roman Britain. Among the complexities to be expected on so long-lived a site are also a huge unfinished court-yard building, temples, workshops, headquar-ters buildings, a length of Stanegate and a monumental fountain fed by an aqueduct. The modern museum (see chapter 8) is excellent, both about the site and in setting it in its context of the frontier of empire.

Planetrees (OS 87: NY 928696). On the south side of B6318 where it begins a steep descent into the North Tyne valley. Be careful about stopping and parking cars here, and be alert for traffic if you are walking along the road.

The short length of Wall displayed here demonstrates narrow (2 metre, 6½ feet) Wall

The Mithraeum, Carrawburgh.

on broad (3 metre, 10 foot) foundations. You can see the same relationship elsewhere. Unless you want to see every single bit of Wall, a visit is hardly worth the traffic risk.

Brunton: turret (26b) (OS 87: NY 922698). On the east side of A6079 between Chollerford and the village of Wall; there is a lay-by.

A short length of Wall up to 2.4 metres (8 feet) high is 'broad' west of a turret on relatively low-lying land looking up the North Tyne valley, and 'narrow' east of it.

Chesters: bridge abutment (OS 87: NY 915700). No vehicular access, so park well back from Chollerford bridge north or south of the river North Tyne. A fenced path leads south-west for about 500 yards from the south end of the bridge.

The monumental remains of the Roman bridge abutment now embedded in the east bank of the river North Tyne incorporate evidence of two bridges: a pier of a ten-pier, timber Hadrianic bridge, and the bulk of the visible abutment which formed the base of the east end of a probably three-arched bridge with a gate tower built early in the third century. The ruin looks more complicated because a leat, perhaps for a mill, was inserted through the base of the tower late in the Roman period.

Chesters: fort (*Cilurnum*) and museum (OS 87: NY 912702). Turn south into the car park off B6318 ⅝ mile west of Chollerford bridge.

At one level Chesters consists of unconnected and not very meaningful bits and pieces of a Roman fort; but it is very much a site to linger over and savour. It is set in mature parkland on the west bank of the North Tyne; one of the best views of it is from the bridge abutment on the east bank.

Apparently scattered in the grass but actually inside a fort are separately excavated gateways (with the Wall itself running off from the west one), corner and interval towers around the unexcavated fort walls, barrack blocks, the commanding officer's house with its private bath-house, and the headquarters building. Outside the east gate is an exposed fragment of the Wall and, beyond, one of the best preserved buildings of Roman Britain, the communal bath-house for the soldiers.

An extensive civil settlement lies around the fort, masked by the undulations of ridge and furrow from arable use of this land before the park was laid out in the early nineteenth century by the Clayton family. The Clayton Collection of material from Chesters and elsewhere along the Wall occupies a purpose-built museum designed by Norman Shaw early in the twentieth century (see chapter 8). It and the internal decor and arrangements are now being maintained as a period piece in their own right.

Black Carts: wall and turret (29a) (OS 87: NY 884714). Turn north off B6318 2 miles west of Chesters on to the minor road to Simonburn. No provision for parking, and turning difficult.

18

The Wall is on both sides of this road. The length on the east contains a turret, from the top of which there would have been a particularly fine view up the river North Tyne.

Carrawburgh: fort (*Brocolitia*), Mithraeum and Coventina's Well (OS 87: NY 859712). Car park on the south side of B6318.

The fort has barely been excavated and is deliberately kept by its private owner as grass-covered earthworks for future research. Visitors who respect this intention are welcome to look over the site, which gives a good idea of what many of the now displayed forts would have looked like for hundreds of years after the Roman period.

Follow the path round the south-east of the fort to the Mithraeum, preserved because it became embedded in a peat bog until its discovery and excavation about 1950. Wood and wickerwork were preserved in these very wet conditions so the detail of posts and bench edges, though now represented by concrete, is correct. The altars are copies. The originals, together with all the material excavated including the sculptures, are in the Museum of Antiquities, Newcastle (see chapter 8), which also contains a full-scale reconstruction of the interior of the Mithraeum.

Sewingshields: Wall, milecastles (34-6) and turrets (OS 87: NY 823705 to 791690). This is a 2½ mile walk with no vehicular access so leave the car at one end or the other, either off B6318 east at the first grid reference or at Housesteads car park.

The main interest is simply to experience the line of the Wall as it climbs up on to the crags of the Whin Sill, with an increasing drop and a magnificent view to the north. The foundations of turret 33b, abandoned in the later second century, are at the east end of this stretch, just west of the point where the B6318 departs from the line of the Wall; milecastle 35, west of Sewing Shields Farm, has been excavated and consolidated for display (with not entirely happy results). It is perched above a vertical crag and now has no north gateway; it was reoccupied in medieval times when it was used as a farm. The much robbed Wall has been consolidated to either side of it. The sites of the other milecastles and turrets along this whole length can be found if looked for because they occur at the standard distances apart. The line of the Wall drops down to the Knag Burn as it approaches Housesteads; to its south, on the east of the burn, are the remains of a native settlement and the boundaries of small rectangular fields of Roman or earlier date.

Housesteads (*Vercovicium*): Wall, fort, civil settlement, field systems, museum and visitor centre (OS 87: NY 790687). Car park on north side of B6318, approached from A69 by A6079 via Chollerford or by minor roads north from Haydon Bridge or Haltwhistle. ⅝ mile walk from car park to fort.

Housesteads is the most visited of the Wall sites and it is not difficult to understand why. In landscape of considerable grandeur, the site itself is an extensive complex of a fort in its context with impressive walks along the Wall to both east and west. Furthermore, the visitor is well served by an excellent National Trust Visitor Centre and a very good English Heritage site museum (see chapter 8). A set of educational rooms has also been opened in the adjacent farm buildings.

The fort itself is bounded by 2-3 metre (6½-10 feet) high walls, with all four gateways excavated. The southern one was used as a house by moss troopers (the local euphemism for highwaymen and rustlers) in the seven-

The line of the Wall along Steel Rigg, Hotbank Crags and, in the far distance, Sewingshields.

teenth century; the western one shows at ground level the mason's lines scored into the stones to ensure a good fit at its front and, in its sides, the holes for the bar which slotted into place when the gate was closed. Inside are the usual accoutrements of a Roman fort, though less than half of the interior has been excavated. In the north-east corner the stone foundations of fourth-century barrack blocks look depressingly similar to modern counterparts. Also familiar but not at all depressing is the communal latrine in the south-east corner, a reminder of Roman skill in making water work and that the privacy of our lavatories is a recent development.

Outside the fort there was settlement beside the streets beyond all the gates but the north, the earthworks outside the west gate being particularly intriguing, while further out still is an extensive spread of field boundaries and cultivation terraces accrued over some two thousand years of agriculture here. (For the walk to the east see the previous entry for Sewingshields; for the walk to the west see Cuddy's Crag below).

Cuddy's Crag to Steel Rigg: Wall, milecastles, turrets, vallum and Roman military way (OS 87: NY 788688 to 751676). Start from either the Housesteads car park and walk west, leaving from the north-west corner of the fort, or from the Steel Rigg car park, approached by the minor road from Twice Brewed on B6318, and walk east. There are no car parks in between and the Wall is inaccessible by vehicle between these two points, 3 miles apart. Access to and from the Wall on foot is possible from the B6318 along the track to Hotbanks Farm about halfway along this stretch.

This length of the frontier is the most popular for those who want to walk a part of the Wall without undertaking a great trek; it now has the advantage of being part of the Pennine Way too. Scenically, the stretch is superb, for the Wall skims along the top of the Whin Sill with its vertical drop and wide views to the north, perhaps at its best overlooking Crag Lough and switchbacking along Peel Crags past milecastle 39.

Archaeologically, all the elements are here, including a native settlement at Milking Gap on the west of the Hotbanks track; the vallum, best seen either side of that track a little further south towards the B6318; and the Roman service road skilfully trying to keep a reasonably level route along a necessarily sinuous course some way back from the Wall itself. A totally unexpected turret was found in Peel Gap (NY 753675) between turrets 39a and 39b by National Trust archaeologists carrying out excavation before consolidation necessitated by the tramp of tourist feet. It too is being preserved as an added point of interest on an already breathtaking stretch of Wall and countryside. Milecastle 37, only a short walk west from Housesteads, is also being excavated and consolidated by the Trust.

Steel Rigg to Cawfields: Wall, milecastles, turrets and vallum (OS 87: NY 751676 to 713666). It is best to start from one car park and walk to the other: from Steel Rigg (see previous entry) walk west to Cawfields, or from the latter walk east. The minor road to Cawfields is signposted north off B6318 at the Milecastle Inn. In between these two points (2½ miles apart) access can be by the minor road north off B6318 to Melkridge Common.

West of Steel Rigg the Wall climbs to its highest point on Winshields Crags (1130 feet, 345 metres, above sea level). It then drops for the narrow pass with the minor road immediately north of Shield on the Wall farm, on either side of which are the best preserved and most dramatic lengths of vallum, and then climbs again on to Thorny Doors, where it survives in one of its highest portions, and then Cawfields Crags. Three milecastles (40, 41, 42) are visible on this stretch, the westernmost (42) clearly visible from the south on an awkward slope just east of a modern quarry. Between it and the B6318, on either side of the minor road leading to the car park, are the banks and ditches of at least four different Roman military enclosures and other earthworks dating from before, during and after the Roman period.

Cawfields to Walltown Crags (OS 87, to western edge: NY 713666 to 670662): Wall, fort, milecastles (44, 45) and turrets (44b, 45a). Walk west from Cawfields car park along the Pennine Way (waymarked) or approach from the west from Greenhead by the minor road north off B6318 past Carvoran fort (and Roman Army Museum).

Great Chesters fort (*Aesica*) is not displayed and is in part occupied by a working farm, but its site, particularly on the west, and its south gate are clearly visible. Westwards the line of the Wall is broken by quarrying, but good lengths stand on Walltown Crags and either side of turret 45a, originally built as a free-standing tower.

The next length (OS 86), from north of Greenhead to the county boundary at Gilsland, is not so impressive but it can be walked and it is a vital stretch in terms of Roman intentions and engineering. Here the Wall crosses the watershed between the Tilpalt Burn, flowing into the Tyne basin, and the river Irthing, running west to Carlisle. The following stretch, just in Cumbria, is one of particular interest, leading to the developing showpiece fort of Birdoswald (*Camboglanna*).

Chesterholm (*Vindolanda*): fort, civil settlement, milestone, museum and reconstructions (OS 87: NY 770664). Approached by minor roads from both A69 at Bardon Mill and Henshaw and the B6318 west of Housesteads.

Like Corbridge, this site is not on the Wall itself but originated as one of the forts on the earlier frontier along the Stanegate. The milestone is beside that road north-east of the fort.

The fort walls and part of the interior are well preserved and displayed in traditional fashion. Archaeologically and visually, the main interest attaches to the extensive excavated remains of the civil settlement outside the west gate. To their south are two genuine tombs and modern full-size models of stone and turf walls. The museum contains displays of the famous *Vindolanda* writing tablets.

5
Churches and other ecclesiastical buildings

The county includes some fine abbeys and priories and a nationally important assemblage of parts of Anglo-Saxon churches; and many of its country churches are interesting, often small, buildings in attractive and peaceful places. Yet, Lindisfarne, Tynemouth and Norham apart, and leaving Hexham, Bywell, Ovingham and their like in a special category, there is little of major academic architectural importance in the ecclesiastical buildings of Northumberland, especially for the medieval period. To paraphrase Pevsner, whereas the history of English castles can be written from the county, the architectural history of English churches could be written with scarcely a reference to Northumberland. Post-medieval revivalist architecture and the architecture of nonconformity are well represented, however, and a small sample is indicated here.

Ancroft: St Anne.

Here is an unusual conjunction of a defensive tower, like a pele tower and probably of about 1300, built into the west end of a Norman church. Remains of the former extent of the village are clear and well preserved, particularly south across the road.

Bolam: St Andrew.

This church has largely lost its village, the earthworks of which extend to the west with prehistoric remains, the agger of the Roman Devil's Causeway and well defined ridge and furrow to the south. The main interest of the church is its late Anglo-Saxon west tower; it also has a good Norman-style interior.

Brinkburn Priory, Longframlington. Telephone: 066570 628. English Heritage. Signposted off the A1 north of Morpeth.

A delightfully peaceful, tucked-away site beside the river Coquet, this Augustinian priory, founded about 1135, retains, as heavily restored in 1858, its church of about 1200 complete and still in use for worship. The remains of a gatehouse lie downstream across the lawn but otherwise only fragments of the priory survive. The attractive adjacent house is

externally of two periods in the first half of the nineteenth century, and presumably the small landscaped garden is contemporary.

Bywell: St Andrew.

The west tower is of fine Anglo-Saxon work with characteristic small round-headed windows; its two structural phases may both be earlier than AD 1000. The rest of the church is mainly thirteenth-century and nineteenth-century restoration. Part of an Anglo-Saxon cross-shaft is in the chancel; stone coffin lids decorate the outside of the north transept.

Brinkburn Priory church.

St Andrew's church, Bywell.

Bywell: St Peter.

St Peter's is of the later eleventh or early twelfth century (the nave) and the thirteenth century, with a fourteenth-century chapel on the north.

Cullercoats: St George.

The tall spire and idealised medieval bulk of this bold Victorian (1884) eyecatcher by J. L. Pearson enliven in a surprisingly appropriate manner the sweep of two-storey Cullercoats Bay, backed behind the church by a cul-de-sac of slightly later and quite classy residences.

Embleton: Holy Trinity.

A good example for Northumberland of a basically medieval interior, with arcades of the late Norman or Early English period between the nave and fifteenth-century aisles, this church is worth visiting for three other reasons: it has strong family connections, in this case with the Greys of Fallodon and the Crasters; the site is a good example of the typical Northumbrian arrangement of church and adjacent vicar's pele, here of about 1400;

and the guidebook, written by a Craster and produced locally, is one of the best about a parish church in the county.

Hexham Abbey (more correctly the Priory Church).

St Wilfrid built the first church here in the AD 670s; an apse and the crypt survive, the latter a complex structure perhaps reflecting origins in the eastern Mediterranean. The church was refounded as part of the priory of Augustinian canons in 1113, though most of the present fabric dates from the late twelfth or early thirteenth century and the later nineteenth century. The obtrusive east front by Dobson is of 1858, but the medieval furnishings inside are the best in the county. Parts of the priory can be discerned with some difficulty in the precinct, which is now municipal rather than monastic in aura. The parish church lay but a short distance away on the south side of the market place up St Mary's Chare.

Hulne Priory, Alnwick.

The priory, which is in Hulne Park, was founded by the Carmelites in about 1240; its ruins now present a reasonably complete picture of a Whitefriars' priory surrounded by its original defensive wall and further protected by a tower of 1488. The whole is now displayed in a picturesque setting enhanced by a Gothick summerhouse of about 1780.

Lindisfarne Priory, Holy Island. English Heritage.

Formerly a cell of the Benedictine monastery at Durham, Lindisfarne Priory now consists of ruins maintained by English Heritage. They comprise the priory church and a complex of monastic buildings; earlier and more extensive structures probably also exist below ground level. The church is renowned for its Norman west front, echoing that of Durham Cathedral, an echo renewed with the massive, decorated piers between the nave and the aisles. To the south, the structures, of the thirteenth century and later, include the fragmentary cloisters and domestic arrangements; beyond them, further south through a gatehouse with a barbican, is an outer court, its high wall and gate to the outer world reminders of defensive needs on Holy Island.

Immediately west of the priory is the parish church of St Mary, a fine building mainly of the late twelfth and thirteenth centuries. The whole is likely to have been within the area of the unlocated Columban monastery founded by St Aidan, who came from Iona in AD 635, and sacked by the Vikings in AD 875.

Morpeth: Presbyterian churches.

On the corner of Copper Chare and Collingwood Lane is the former Presbyterian church of about 1732, an early date. Its successor (1860) dominates the east end of Bridge Street and the New Bridge with its tower and short, octagonal spire.

Newminster Abbey. Between Morpeth and Mitford on the banks of the river Wansbeck.

The ruins of a Cistercian abbey founded in 1137 are much robbed, partly overgrown, very partially excavated and partly, if confusingly, restored.

Norham: St Cuthbert.

With Lindisfarne and Tynemouth priories, Norham is the most important Norman ecclesiastical building in Northumberland. It lies impressively at the west end of the village that developed below the castle of the Bishops of Durham. As at Durham Cathedral itself, the south arcade is of bulky circular piers while externally the striking aspect is the array of arcaded and shafted windows along the south side of the chancel. Much of the rest of the building is of about 1850.

North Shields: nonconformist churches.

The growth of the town in the early nineteenth century included the building of numerous nonconformist churches and chapels. Many survive and are interesting both in their own right and as parts of a self-consciously stylish urban fabric, for example, in Howard Street, the Scotch Church (1811) and the Baptist church 1846, both by Dobson, together with a former Methodist church of 1856 beside the Town Hall and a former Wesleyan church of 1807; and in Northumberland Square, centre of the new town at the

north end of Howard Street, St Columba's Presbyterian church, also by Dobson (1850-7).

Old Bewick: Holy Trinity.

An isolated church in a secluded spot beside a stream, it consists of a small nave and a chancel with an original and still visible apse. The arches to chancel and apse are splendidly Norman, and indeed the whole church seems to be remarkably untouched since the twelfth century. It was, however, repaired in 1695 and in the mid nineteenth century.

Ovingham: St Mary.

The tall late Anglo-Saxon west tower, with original windows, forms a satisfying composition with a mainly thirteenth-century church. Thomas Bewick was buried here.

Tynemouth Priory (OS 88: NZ 374695). English Heritage.

The priory lies within the castle, on a headland overlooking the mouth of the river Tyne and very impressive in profile when floodlit by English Heritage. The site was occupied in late prehistoric times and, contemporaneously with Jarrow and Monkwearmouth south of the river, was marked by an Anglo-Saxon monastery from the seventh century AD. Sacked by the Vikings, its warlike connections continue into the twentieth century with a First World War coastal battery (the magazine of which has been reconstructed) and military occupation until 1960.

The headland is cut off by an Elizabethan curtain wall, comparable with the contemporary defences of Berwick, dominated by a huge gatehouse completed about 1400. Most of the rest of the castle has disappeared. Its walls

Tynemouth Priory.

were nearly 1070 yards (975 metres) in circuit; when the monastery was suppressed in 1539, the castle was retained by the Crown for the defence of the realm.

The priory is best represented by the church, built about 1100; the west door is impressive and the walls of the presbytery stand to above window level.

Foundations of other buildings survive or are marked out in the grass but a copy of the site plan is needed to appreciate the range and complexity of the monastic establishment. The fifteenth-century Percy Chantry has a splendid ceiling.

Warden: St Michael.

In many ways this church is architecturally typical for Northumberland, and hence its inclusion here, but it also typically possesses its own special local interest. It is idyllically situated with its vicarage close to the confluence of the North and South Tyne rivers, almost hidden away down a cul-de-sac and set in a maturely wooded graveyard. The west tower is of late Anglo-Saxon type but perhaps of about 1100 rather than 1000. It was used for beacons warning of border raids and is surmounted with an addition of 1765. Much of the medieval church was rebuilt then, largely financed by the Blacketts of Wallington, and the chancel was medievalised in Victorian style

in 1889. The Clayton Chapel represents the family interests of the Claytons of Chesters, of whom John Clayton did so much to preserve and cultivate interest in Hadrian's Wall from 1822 onwards. Appropriately then, inside the church, in the porch, and outside, are several decorated stones of considerable archaeological interest.

Warkworth Hermitage, Warkworth. English Heritage.

This may not be the greatest of medieval buildings in the care of English Heritage but it is rewarding to visit it because either you have to walk along the beautiful south bank of the river Coquet from Warkworth and attract the custodian's attention to ferry you across or, better still, you hire a boat below the castle and row yourself to the hermitage: surely the way it was meant to be approached.

Woodhorn Church, Ashington. Telephone: 0670 817371.

A village church, restored in 1842 and again more recently but with original early Norman features, it survives as an isolated old building in an area disfigured by the mining of coal. It now houses a small museum, including two fragments of an Anglo-Saxon cross-shaft and temporary exhibitions, surrounded by modestly pleasant grounds including a picnic area.

St Michael and All Angels, Warden.

The entrance to Alnwick Castle.

6
Castles and fortifications

Northumberland's claim to be the county of castles is well founded: there are about five hundred of them. They range from the magnificence of maintained and still occupied castles like that of the Duke of Northumberland at Alnwick to unrecognised and overgrown heaps of stones or names in documents unattached to anything on the ground.

The county had been frontier country long before the time of the Norman Conquest and many defensive structures had been built over the centuries; yet it was only after 1066 that the first proper castles were planted by the conquerors. By 1100 many of the castles whose names are familiar to us were in existence, including Newcastle itself, Alnwick, Bamburgh, Norham, Prudhoe and Warkworth. At that stage they were without the elaboration of stone fortifications, which in general were added later, and at some early castles which did not develop we can still see the original motte and bailey design, for example at Elsdon.

Central towers called keeps were added to some of the early castles, particularly during the civil war of the mid twelfth century. New castles appeared too as local warlords strove to establish ascendancy among their peers as much as to challenge royal authority and

defend themselves against the Scots. Northumberland was very much disputed territory in the later twelfth and earlier thirteenth centuries, being part of Scotland for a time before finally coming under the English Crown; but that formality did not stop the fourteenth century being one of continual warfare. Castles came to be characterised by high surrounding walls but they proved vulnerable to sappers, hence the development of corner towers to strengthen the weakest points and interval towers to fire along the walls. Castles became sitting targets with the advent of cannon, however, and the resultant rethink is eloquently expressed in Berwick's town defences.

Some castles, like Aydon, were really fortified houses. Many other residences were also made defensible at least for a time. This was done generally in one of three ways. The most military-looking were the tower houses like Belsay and Chipchase. Though Ford and Chillingham were built to a different plan they are essentially of the same type — a major domestic residence capable of being defended. They can be regarded as small castles and were certainly meant to be seen as such in the fourteenth and fifteenth centuries.

As an alternative, but a matter of degree

rather than something completely different, so-called pele towers were often added to existing houses, particularly in the fourteenth century and later. Sometimes, however, these towers were new, free-standing structures. They had thick walls and few entrances and provided animal stalling at ground level, with domestic quarters on the first and second floors. Survivors are scattered about Northumberland, the best preserved often being 'vicar's peles' still standing close to a church. Corbridge and Elsdon are good examples, both of them visitable.

The other main type of defensive building, characteristically at farmhouse level rather than higher up the social scale, is the bastle. This too has animal accommodation at ground level, with living space on a first floor approached by outside steps. Compared to peles, which had walls of equal height all round to make a square tower, the bastles are usually rectangular in plan with pointed gables at the narrower ends to take a pitched roof. In other words, a bastle is a substantially built, rectangular stone house, modified to provide some protection to a farming family and its stock, probably in the sixteenth and seventeenth centuries.

Some castles, such as Newcastle, saw action again in the English Civil War of the 1640s. Many were ruinous by then and indeed had been a century earlier according to a survey by Henry VIII. Now, however, many are well looked after in private hands while others are cared for, to the public benefit, by the National Trust and English Heritage.

Alnwick Castle, Alnwick. Telephone: 0665 602207.

The home of the Percys from 1309 to the mid eighteenth century, and thereafter of the Dukes of Northumberland, this is the most distinguished of the Northumbrian castles. It now overlooks to the north and east sedate parkland by 'Capability' Brown and to the south and west, its medieval market town. The castle has a long and complex structural history, beginning in the eleventh century with the motte and bailey castle of Yvo de Vescy, the first Norman Baron of Alnwick. This was replaced in the twelfth century by the circular stone shell keep which still forms the core of the main buildings around a small inner court and between two outer baileys. A major phase of restoration occurred in 1854-65 under the Victorian architect Salvin.

As well as the principal apartments, the castle contains a great art collection, an important archaeological museum and a highly proficient archive much used for historical research into the lives and estates of one of England's premier families.

Permits to walk in adjacent Hulne Park can be obtained from the Estates Office at the castle.

Aydon Castle (OS 87: NZ 002664). Telephone: 043471 2450. English Heritage. Signposted east off A68 north of Corbridge or north off B6321 just north-east of the village of Aydon.

Essentially a fortified house with two baileys, it occupies a locally strong and attractive position on a spur above a steep-sided wooded valley on three sides. The site has been restored by English Heritage and opened to the public. The house, already a two-storeyed hall in stone, was fortified about 1300 to meet the Scottish threat but apparently to no avail as it was seized by the Scots in 1315 and by English rebels in 1317. However, it remains remarkably unaltered as a medieval country house. It became a farm in the

Black Middens Bastle, Tarset.

Dunstanburgh Castle.

seventeenth century and continued as such until modern times.

Bamburgh Castle, Bamburgh. Telephone: 06684 208.

The situation is unequalled in England in its drama for the castle crowns an outcrop of near-vertical Whin Sill rock seaward of the coastline proper, giving it superb views north over beaches and dunes to Lindisfarne, east to the Farne Islands, south along the coast towards Dunstanburgh and inland to Cheviot. This rock was occupied in prehistoric times and was probably the seat of the early kings of Northumbria from the sixth century AD. The present fortifications begin with the twelfth-century keep, around which three baileys were formed; but the well known and visually impressive castle profile, so effectively flood-lit, is largely the result of extensive restoration and building work in the mid eighteenth century and, more particularly, in the late nineteenth century by the first Lord Armstrong (of Vickers Armstrong).

Bellister Castle, Haltwhistle NE49 0HZ. Telephone: 0498 20391.

The historical centre of the National Trust's 1100 acre (445 ha) Bellister estate, the ruined medieval pele tower may be visited by appointment with the tenant. The castle was added in the seventeenth century and considerably altered in the early nineteenth century.

Berwick-upon-Tweed fortifications

The town walls, begun by Edward I in 1296 to defend England's most northerly town (a claim frequently disputed by the Scots), are of international importance for their later development. They are the earliest example in northern Europe, and the only example in England (or Scotland), of Italian Renaissance fortification, the result of major redesign and additions in 1558-66 to combat artillery. A text-book example of the latest in military thinking at the time, they are splendidly preserved and invite, literally, circumambulation. They are accessible at all times.

Black Middens Bastle, Tarset. English Heritage. 3 miles north of Bellingham. Signposted from B6320.

A classic example of the Northumbrian bastle, this defensive, sixteenth-century house consists of a ground floor entered through the east gable, an outside stone staircase on the south wall, and a first-floor living room originally with wooden flooring and a hearth against the west gable. It is accessible at all times.

The ruins of a similar building lie immediately east, and the approach to the site up the Tarset valley passes two other bastles at Gatehouse.

Dunstanburgh Castle. Telephone: 066576 231. National Trust and English Heritage. Accessible only on foot either along the edge of the golf course from Embleton to the north or along the coastal path from Craster to the south.

Many people's favourite castle because of its isolated position above the sea and its romantic aspect, Dunstanburgh consists of a fortified gatehouse on the south, later bypassed with a new entrance on the north, an inner ward with domestic buildings, and a large, apparently empty, walled bailey. The area enclosed (11 acres, 4.5 ha) makes it the most extensive of the Northumbrian castles. It was a Lancastrian stronghold, begun in 1313 and much involved during the Wars of the Roses; it was badly damaged by cannon, for instance in a siege of 1464. It seems never to have been fully repaired and has been in decay for over five hundred years. A failed harbour lies below it inland on its west.

Edlingham Castle, Edlingham. English Heritage. Situated between Alnwick and Rothbury on a minor road off B6341.

In a valley dominated by a viaduct, the site catches the eye with its tower; but this is of the fifteenth century, added to a thirteenth-century moated hall-house defended from about 1300 onwards by a gatehouse and walls. The site has been excavated and displayed by English Heritage.

Earthworks of a former part of the village lie to the south-west towards the church, which also has a defensible tower.

Elsdon Castle. On the north-east edge of Elsdon village.

The best of the purely earthwork castles in Northumberland, it consists of a motte and bailey with still impressive ditches perched above the narrow pass into the village down the Elsdon Burn from the north. It represents the classic Norman fortification imposed on the landscape soon after the Conquest, here uncluttered by later accretions of a developed castle.

Etal Castle. English Heritage. At the end of Etal village street off B6354, signposted from A697 between Wooler and Cornhill.

The gatehouse facing down the street is part of a walled circuit partly preserved among farm buildings and enclosing a fourteenth-century tower house, the whole overlooking a former bridge, ford and ferry across the river Till. The castle was already 'greatly decayed' in 1564.

Langley Castle. Telephone: 043484 8888. Beside A686 about 1¼ miles south of A69 near Haydon Bridge.

Externally Langley Castle is very impressive as a mid fourteenth-century tower house with four projecting angle towers and a stair tower on the east face. The ruinous castle was heavily restored around 1900 in the fashion of the time by Cadwallader Bates and, now a late Victorian period piece in its own right, it specialises in medieval banquets.

Newcastle Castle. See under Newcastle upon Tyne, The Keep Museum (chapter 8).

Norham Castle. Telephone: 028982 329. English Heritage. On top of the hill at the east end of Norham village by A698.

Situated in a very strong natural position overlooking a ford across the river Tweed, this castle belonged, perhaps rather surprisingly, to the Bishops of Durham. It was started in the twelfth century with a motte and keep and was thereafter constantly in the wars between the English and the Scots. With a reputation for

Prudhoe Castle.

impregnability, it finally fell to James IV of Scotland on his way to Flodden. It contains some interesting Tudor work from its sixteenth-century rebuilding. As important, architecturally and militarily as better known Northumbrian castles, like Warkworth it also has an interesting relationship with its 'town'.

Preston Tower, Chathill NE67 5DH. Telephone: 066 589227.

The remains of a late fourteenth-century tower house with four corner towers are set in an informal atmosphere created by charming gardens, to which visitors are welcome. Originally built by Robert Harbottle, Sheriff of Northumberland and Constable of Dunstanburgh, the structure was significantly reduced in the seventeenth century. The tower now visible, consisting of two towers linked by a stairwell, is the remnant as partly rebuilt in the mid nineteenth century. The magnificent clock and the water tanks to serve the new farm and house were installed in 1864. Otherwise the interior is now used unpretentiously to convey something of the atmosphere and history of a fortified border home from which a Harbottle went forth to his death on Flodden Field.

Prudhoe Castle. Telephone: 0228 31777. English Heritage. Overlooking the bridge at Ovingham between A69 and A695.

The immediate setting and the castle itself are impressive. Like Aydon, the castle has been consolidated and opened by English Heritage. It is well worth visiting, for it is visibly one of Northumberland's great castles (about which there is also a small exhibition). It came to the Percys in 1381 when its twelfth-century keep and gatehouse were already old, and it maintained a key position in Border warfare because of its location close to the intersection of the east-west route with a main south-north one. It was nevertheless dilapidated by about 1600 and partly restored by the Duke of Northumberland in the decade from 1808.

Tynemouth Castle. See Tynemouth Priory, chapter 5.

Warkworth Castle. Telephone: 0665 711423. English Heritage. Beside A1068 between Amble and Alnmouth.

Preston Tower.

Warkworth has most of the things expected of a castle. Superbly sited across the neck of land created by a loop in the river Coquet, it overlooks its planned town to the north and the lower reaches of the river to the south-east. Originally a Norman motte and bailey castle, it came to form a pair with Alnwick Castle from early in the fourteenth century when it came into Percy hands. In 1399 it featured in national history when the Percys proclaimed Henry IV king of England here; they still own the castle.

Belsay Hall.

7
Historic houses and gardens

Because of Northumberland's position as a border area, it has not, until relatively recently, been ideally suited to the establishment of country estates destined for peaceful leisured pursuits. Formerly, Northumberland's upper and middle classes lived in fortified residences: aristocracy in castles, gentry in pele towers, farmers in bastles (chapter 6). Many of the larger houses in the Northumberland countryside incorporate earlier fortified tower houses — in 1415 there were 76 recorded pele towers. It was not until the period of enclosure that there began to be a feeling of security sufficient to allow the country house and its customary lifestyle to become a strong cultural influence in the county. Maybe because of this late arrival and the isolation of many estate communities, the feudal way of life is still much in evidence in Northumberland today.

The majority of estates are still in private ownership and consequently the houses and gardens which are regularly open to the public are relatively few. They are listed below.

Belsay Hall and Castle, Belsay. Telephone: 066181 636. English Heritage.

The historic centre of this interesting and diverse estate of the Middleton family is now in the care of English Heritage. The castle, some distance from the hall, is the original dwelling; it is an oblong tunnel-vaulted tower, probably of the fourteenth century. Adjoining it is a house of 1614 with a partially demolished eighteenth-century wing. There was an ornate formal garden in front of the main block. A Victorian model farmyard is to the rear.

Earthworks in the park indicate that there was a settlement in the grounds before the nineteenth century, when the present village, with an elegant arcaded terrace, was built outside the park.

Belsay Hall, built in 1810-17, is one of the most imposing and important neo-classical houses in Britain. Its simple, even austere, Greek-influence design is the work of a member of the Middleton family, Sir Charles Monk; he was assisted by John Dobson. The hall had been empty, though well maintained, for some years before it was acquired by English Heritage. Displayed in an unfurnished state, it is interesting to see the bare bones of a house, particularly one of this nature for which simplicity is a major characteristic.

Not all the grounds are open to the public. The most fascinating portion is the Quarry Garden, with towering rock faces, formed from the quarry from which stone for the hall was obtained.

Cragside House and Country Park, Rothbury, Morpeth NE65 7PX. Telephone: 0669 20333. National Trust.

The home and hobby of the inventor, arms manufacturer and philanthropist Lord Armstrong, the Cragside estate is now in the sympathetic ownership of the National Trust. The stone house garnished with half-timbering is in an Olde English style by Richard Norman Shaw from 1870 to 1895 and incorporates an earlier fishing lodge; its location is a precipitous position on rock, overlooking a splendidly wooded gorge crossed by a delicate steel footbridge (now closed to the public as unsafe) made at Lord Armstrong's Elswick Works in Newcastle. The house has fine glass by William Morris in the library, and it was the first private dwelling to be lit by hydro-electricity. Above all, the house is fascinating as an indicator of the taste and lifestyle of a self-made man of the period.

There is much to see in the grounds, the restoration of which is still in hand. It is advisable to start a visit to Cragside at the visitor centre in the old stable block, where, in the Armstrong Energy Centre, an exhibition introduces Lord Armstrong and his estate. Also in the complex are a good restaurant, a shop and a restored waterwheel brought from one of the Cragside estate farms.

There are walks and a circular drive round the rhododendron-clad hillside to the main points of interest, most of which relate to the hydro-electric system. At the top of the hill are reservoirs and associated stone-lined water conduits. In the woods leading from the house to the Power House at Burn Foot are remnants of the wooden casing for the electric wire, which itself survives in places. The 1½ mile (2.5 km) Power Circuit Walk, starting from the Armstrong Energy Centre, encompasses the Power House and the Ram House and passes reservoirs, bridges and romantic glades along its rock-girt route.

Howick Garden, Howick Hall, Howick NE66 3LB. Telephone: 066577 285.

Renowned for its garden, the classical hall, which is not open to the public, was built in the late eighteenth century to the design of a Newcastle architect, William Newton. It was the home of the Grey family. The second Earl, responsible for the Reform Bill, is commemorated by a noble monument at the top of Grey Street in Newcastle. The hall has been much altered and added to: in 1809 by George Wyatt, and in 1928, after fire required a major reconstruction of the main block, by Sir Herbert Baker (architect, with Edwin Lutyens, of the Indian City of New Delhi).

The woodland garden is 'wild', with a wide range of flowering trees and shrubs, many normally considered too tender for the region. The daffodils and the shrubs, including rhododendrons especially, are the main attraction for visitors. An arboretum is being planted.

On the other side of Howick Burn is the nineteenth-century church.

The sea can be reached by a walk of 1½ miles (2.5 km) through woodland from the hall garden. On the shore a mile north is a Victorian bathing house built for the Greys. Nearby are good rock pools at Rumbling Kern.

Lindisfarne Castle and Garden, Holy Island, Berwick-upon-Tweed TD15 2RH. Telephone: 0289 89244.

This sixteenth-century castle built to protect Holy Island harbour was purchased by the owner of *Country Life* magazine, Edward Hudson. In 1903 he restored it to the design of Edwin Lutyens as a private house. Behind the castle exterior is a cosy small home. Hudson had a good view across the water to the rival castle residence of his fellow plutocrat Lord Armstrong at Bamburgh; perhaps both were playing at being feudal lords. The castle is very popular, so it is advisable to avoid peak visiting times if possible. To the north, across a sweep of grass is the walled garden designed

Cragside.

Lindisfarne Castle.

by Gertrude Jekyll. Despite the local propensity to place a garden some distance from its house, the suburban aspect of the garden and the interior seems out of place on a windswept Northumbrian isle.

Seaton Delaval Hall, Seaton Sluice, Whitley Bay, Tyne and Wear NE26 4QR. Telephone: 091 2731493.

A baroque house of 1718-29 was formed on a Palladian plan of a main block and flanking wings to the design of Sir John Vanbrugh. He died before building was completed. A fire in the east wing in 1752 and another in 1822 have left indelible marks on the interior of the main portion so that it is a shadow of the original concept. The west wing is still a residence and contains furniture and paintings previously dispersed throughout the hall. The park is in a rather unhappy state, being encroached upon by later development. The original grand design rivalled Vanbrugh's other great work, Castle Howard in North Yorkshire, in its use of avenues, pavilions, temples, a mausoleum and such like. Some remnants of the scheme remain, such as the mausoleum and a hand-

Seaton Delaval Hall, north front.

The griffin heads at Wallington Hall.

some obelisk which closes the view to the south.

The farm buildings and a duck pond, near the tree-shaded Norman parish church, form a charming group. At the west end of the western avenue is the sad-looking former coal-mining village of Seaton Delaval (for Seaton Sluice see chapter 11).

Wallington Hall, Cambo, Morpeth NE61 4AR. Telephone: 0670 74283. National Trust.

Enveloping the remains of a seventeenth-century castle, Wallington Hall is a gracious pedimented 1740s house amid a large estate ranging from formal gardens and parkland to rough moorland, all in the ownership of the National Trust. Such is the variety of interest available outdoors that the house has become almost a sideshow. Many visitors come to Wallington to stroll in the gardens and woods or to walk one of the longer trails, like that which follows the old railway track of the 'Wannie Line'. 'Capability' Brown, who was born nearby at Kirkharle, was called in to effect changes to the Wallington landscape in 1769 (see also Rothley Crags in chapter 2).

The route to the hall from the car park leads beneath the handsome clock-tower to a green, with the hall beyond. On each side, adjoining the clock-tower stable block, which houses the

restaurant and shop, are pretty estate cottages and gardens. At the time of the Wallington Festival there are special events such as the popular evening performances of Shakespeare on the west lawn.

The Wallington estate belonged to the mine-owning Blackett family until 1777, when it transferred through inheritance to the Trevelyans, a family of intellect and liberal persuasion who had much influence on house and estate. The hall has fine interiors, especially the eighteenth-century plaster ceilings. Local people, in particular, enjoy the romanticised Victorian murals of Northumbrian history by William Bell Scott in the Central Hall created by John Dobson from an open courtyard. The view from the hall to the south extends across smooth lawns and the unseen ha-ha to parkland leading down to the river Wansbeck. It was formerly dammed to create a lake and is crossed by a beautiful eighteenth-century bridge by James Paine.

A north-south road runs through the Wallington estate. To its east, within the ha-ha, are woods, lakes and gardens. The secluded walled garden and the conservatory there are usually well sheltered from the brisk Northumbrian winds.

Cambo, the estate village of Wallington, is to the north-east (chapter 11).

8
Museums

ALNWICK
Alnwick Castle Museum of Antiquities, Alnwick Castle, Alnwick, NE66 1NQ. Telephone: 0665 510777.

The museum has been open since 1826. There are artefacts from prehistoric, Roman, Celtic and Viking periods, including exhibits from Pompeii.

House of Hardy Museum, Willowburn, Alnwick NE66 2PG. Telephone: 0665 602771.

The museum is on the outskirts of the town, in a smart single-storey neo-classical factory building. It is a mecca for fishermen and armchair fishermen. The history of this famous firm is described, and superb fishing tackle is displayed. There is also clothing for more general country pursuits.

Royal Northumberland Fusiliers Regimental Museum, The Abbot's Tower, Alnwick Castle, Alnwick NE66 1NG. Telephone: 0665 602152.

In this museum there is a display of the regiment's relics and history.

BAMBURGH
Bamburgh Castle and Armstrong Museum, Bamburgh NE69 7DF. Telephone: 06684 208.

In the castle (see chapter 6) there is a collection of arms, armour, tapestries and china. There are also exhibits about the first Lord Armstrong and his inventions.

Grace Darling Museum, 1 Radcliffe Road, Bamburgh NE69 7AE. Telephone: 0665 720037.

The museum contains memorabilia relating to the rescue of survivors from the wrecked *Forfarshire* by Grace Darling and her father. Visitors are not charged for admission but donations to the Royal National Lifeboat Institution are welcomed.

BERWICK-UPON-TWEED
Berwick Barracks, Castle and Ramparts, Berwick-upon-Tweed. Telephone: 0289 304493. English Heritage.

There are three early eighteenth-century barrack blocks and a gatehouse round a square, with an exhibition. A gun tower and the west wall of the castle are open to the public, as is the superb Tudor system of fortifications (see chapter 6).

Berwick-upon-Tweed Borough Museum and Art Gallery, The Clock Block, Berwick Barracks, Ravensdowne, Berwick-upon-Tweed.

Telephone: 0289 308473.

The exhibits cover local history, archaeology and natural history. There is also a display of fine and decorative art which includes a collection given by Sir William Burrell.

King's Own Scottish Borderers Regimental Museum, The Barracks, Berwick-upon-Tweed. Telephone: 0289 307426.

There is a display of uniforms, medals, weapons and silver.

CARVORAN
Roman Army Museum, Carvoran, Greenhead CA6 7JB Telephone: 06972 485.

This museum near Walltown Crags is devoted to the Roman army, with special reference to Hadrian's Wall. There is a large reconstruction of a Roman barrack room. There is a film theatre with frequent film showings. Among educational services available, with advance notice, are a special talk and a guided walk. An unexcavated fort lies next to the museum.

CHESTERHOLM
Chesterholm Museum, Chesterholm, Bardon Mill, Hexham NE47 7JN. Telephone: 0498 4277.

At Chesterholm is the partly excavated site of a Roman fort (*Vindolanda*) and associated civilian settlement (see chapter 4). There are full-size reconstructions of a portion of Hadrian's Wall and a tower. In the museum are artefacts from the site, including remarkable wooden and leather objects preserved because they were deposited in ground which became waterlogged.

CHOLLERFORD
Clayton Memorial Museum, Chesters Roman Fort, Chollerford, Humshaugh, Hexham. Telephone: 043481 379. English Heritage.

This museum houses the collection of the Clayton Trustees, administered by the Department of Archaeology, University of Newcastle upon Tyne. The display style is representative of museum presentation in about 1900 and is itself worthy of study. The Roman site is nearby, on both sides of the South Tyne (see chapter 4).

CORBRIDGE
Corbridge Roman Site Museum, Corbridge. Telephone: 043471 2349. English Heritage.

This English Heritage museum is run in conjunction with the Department of Archaeology of the University of Newcastle and lies

Berwick-upon-Tweed: the Elizabethan ramparts.

within the Roman site. The exhibits in a modern museum building include artefacts and models relating to the Roman fort and supply base at Corbridge. The famous Roman sculpture of the Corbridge Lion is displayed.

FORD
Lady Waterford Gallery, Ford, Berwick-upon-Tweed TD15 2QG. Telephone: 089082 524. For access apply to the curator in Ford village.

The former village school, now the village hall, is famous for its nineteenth-century murals, painted by Louisa, Marchioness of Waterford. She used the local estate workers and their children as models for the figures in the Old and New Testament scenes. There is also a display of some of Lady Waterford's other works and associated articles.

HEXHAM
Middle March Centre for Border History, Manor Office, Hallgate, Hexham NE46 3NH. Telephone: 0434 604011.

The centre houses a display on facets of the life of border dwellers during the constant wars and political tension on the Anglo-Scottish border in medieval and Tudor times.

HOUSESTEADS
Housesteads Roman Fort Museum and Information Centre, Haydon Bridge, Hexham. Telephone: 04984 363. National Trust and English Heritage.

The site and museum belong to the National Trust but both are staffed by English Heritage. The Trust has opened a teaching room at the farm near the fort and runs a combined information centre and shop near the car park in a building resembling a Northumbrian farm hemel. On display are finds from the Roman fort and the civilian settlement outside.

KILLINGWORTH
Stephenson Railway Museum, Dial Cottage, Great Lime Road, Killingworth, Newcastle upon Tyne. See under North Shields, below.

LINDISFARNE
Lindisfarne Priory Museum, Holy Island, Lindisfarne. Telephone: 028989 200. English Heritage.

In the museum is a display telling with excellent graphics and some objects the complicated history of Lindisfarne and its priory.

MICKLEY
Thomas Bewick Birthplace Trust, Cherryburn, Mickley, Stocksfield NE43 7DB. Telephone: 0661 843276.

In a beautiful location overlooking the river Tyne, Cherryburn, the birthplace of the engraver and naturalist Thomas Bewick (1753-1828), was opened to the public in 1988. There is an exhibition of Bewick's life and work in the main house, to the accompaniment of the Northumbrian small-pipes. The birthplace itself is charmingly restored and furnished, the main room appearing as depicted in a drawing by Thomas Bewick's son Robert. There is a cobbled farmyard with outbuildings, cattle, sheep, geese, ducks, hens and a pig. Frequent printing demonstrations of Bewick's wood engravings are given in the printing house.

MORPETH
Morpeth Chantry Bagpipe Museum, The Chantry, Bridge Street, Morpeth NE61 1PJ. Telephone: 0670 519466.

This much praised museum, in a medieval building, tells the story of bagpipes and their music, including the Northumbrian small-pipes.

Morpeth Old Chantry School houses the Bagpipe Museum.

NEWCASTLE UPON TYNE

Blackfriars Centre, Monk Street, Newcastle upon Tyne NE1 4XW. Telephone: 091 2615367.

The centre is in the restored buildings of the thirteenth-century Dominican friary. The complex includes a museum, craft centre, tourist information centre and restaurant. There are a pleasant courtyard and garden with the layout of excavated buildings defined on the ground. The story of Newcastle is well told in an exhibition, with audio-visual displays, upstairs.

Greek Museum, Percy Building, The University, Newcastle upon Tyne NE1 7RU. Telephone: 091 2226000, extension 7966.

This small museum holds a fine collection of Greek and Etruscan antiquities, with special emphasis on painted vases, terracottas and metalwork, including armour.

Hancock Museum, Barras Bridge, Newcastle upon Tyne NE2 4PT. Telephone: 091 2227418.

This handsome museum, purpose-built in 1878, is administered by the University of Newcastle upon Tyne and the Natural History Society of Northumbria. Displayed in the galleries is a comprehensive collection, imaginatively presented. Interesting displays relate to Northumbrian wildlife and geology, with a whole room full of John Hancock's spectacular birds. The trophies collected by the big-game hunter Abel Chapman peer from the portholes of an 'ark'. The ethnographic exhibits are

especially impressive. There is a small exhibition on the local engraver and naturalist Thomas Bewick (see also Mickley, above).

Hatton Gallery, The Quadrangle, The University, Newcastle upon Tyne NE1 7RU. Telephone: 091 2226000 extension 6059 or 6057.

The gallery, in an elegant location, houses an eclectic permanent collection of paintings and drawings. There is a programme of temporary exhibitions and a diary of other events such as lunchtime discussions.

John George Joicey Museum, City Road, Newcastle upon Tyne NE1 2AS. Telephone: 091 2324562.

Of principal interest is the museum building, splendid arcaded seventeenth-century almshouses of brick with stone moulding. The interior has been skilfully utilised to house room sets and exhibits relating to the city of Newcastle. There is also military material, which includes the Regimental Museum of the 15th/19th The King's Royal Hussars and the defunct Northumberland Hussars.

The Keep Museum, St Nicholas Street, Newcastle upon Tyne NE1 1RQ. Telephone: 091 2327938.

The museum is curated by the Society of Antiquaries of Newcastle upon Tyne and is housed in Henry II's 'New Castle' of 1170, which provides a good panorama of the city of Newcastle and the river Tyne. There is a

Above: *The Military Vehicle Museum in the Exhibition Park Pavilion, Newcastle upon Tyne.*

Below: *The arcaded almshouses forming the John George Joicey Museum in Newcastle upon Tyne.*

display on the history of the castle, which was separated from its Black Gate when the railway was built between the two.

Laing Art Gallery, Higham Place, Newcastle upon Tyne NE1 8AG. Telephone: 091 2327734.

This is the region's major art gallery. It houses a collection of paintings, silver, glass, ceramics and textiles. Temporary exhibitions are also held.

Military Vehicle Museum, Exhibition Park Pavilion, Newcastle upon Tyne NE2 4PZ. Telephone: 091 2817222.

A collection created by the North Military Vehicle Club is located in the last remaining pavilion of the 1929 North-east Coast Exhibition. There is special emphasis on Second World War vehicles and militaria.

Museum of Antiquities, The University, Newcastle upon Tyne NE1 7RU. Telephone: 091 2227844 or 2226000.

This is the major archaeological museum in the North-east. The basis of its display is the collection of the Society of Antiquaries of Newcastle upon Tyne. The material exhibited ranges from the prehistoric to the post-medieval period. The museum is a good starting point for those wishing to find out about Hadrian's Wall; many of the most important antiquities from the Wall are here. There is a model of the whole length of the Wall, and a walk-in reconstruction of the

Sundial and inscription above the front door, Dial Cottage, Killingworth, the home of George and Robert Stephenson.

Carrawburgh Mithraeum with an audio-visual presentation. There are occasional temporary exhibitions.

Museum of Science and Engineering, Blandford House, Blandford Square, Newcastle upon Tyne NE1 4JA. Telephone: 091 2326789.

The splendid displays give a good introduction to Tyneside's important industrial history. There is a telling wall model of Tyneside in 1929.

Newcastle Polytechnic Gallery, Library Building, Sandyford Road, Newcastle upon Tyne NE1 8ST. Telephone: 091 2326002.

There is a continuing programme of exhibitions of the work of contemporary international artists.

Trinity Maritime Centre, 29 Broad Chare, Quayside, Newcastle upon Tyne NE1 3DQ. Telephone: 091 2614691.

Displays of maritime history are housed in an early Victorian warehouse off one of the old streets, or 'chares', leading from the Quayside.

NORTH SHIELDS

Stephenson Railway Museum Project, Middle Engine Lane, North Shields, Tyne and Wear. Telephone: 091 2622627.

The project will eventually encompass a Stephenson museum at Dial Cottage, Great Lime Road, Killingworth (the home of the Stephensons, George and Robert), linked to the Middle Engine Lane museum by a Killingworth Wagon Walk. Another walk will lead from Dial Cottage around wagonways in the area. Meanwhile, there is limited opening only. Dial Cottage, in a small terrace, is charming; the sundial over the door was put up by the Stephensons in 1816. Their first locomotive was made close by. This pretty spot conveys an impression of how pleasantly rural were many parts of Tyneside, notwithstanding the presence of industry.

WALLSEND

Wallsend Heritage Centre, 2 Buddle Street, Wallsend, Tyne and Wear NE28 6EH. Telephone: 091 2620012.

The heritage centre overlooks the Tyne, alongside the Roman fort of *Segedunum*, finds from which are displayed as part of the presentation of the history of Wallsend from the Roman period, when it was the easternmost point of Hadrian's Wall. Exhibits encompass facets of Wallsend's important industrial past, notably shipbuilding. Down the road on the shore is the working shipyard of Swan Hunter. The layout of the Roman fort (see chapter 4) is delineated on site, immediately to the south-west of the heritage centre; its commanding position is immediately apparent.

WYLAM

George Stephenson's Birthplace, Wylam NE41 8BP. Telephone: 06614 3457.

This mid eighteenth-century cottage east of Wylam is approached on foot along the track of the old railway, called the Wylam and Wallbottle Wagonway. The parlour of the cottage where Stephenson, the railway pioneer, was born in 1781 looks as it might have done in the late nineteenth century. Railways, or wagonways, had evolved on Tyneside in response to the need to haul coal in trucks from the mines to points on the river Tyne for transfer to water transport. Stephenson saw the potential of the locomotive, the moving engine, for this purpose.

Site of the battle of Heavenfield, AD 634.

9
Other places to visit

Bardon Mill Pottery, Errington Reay and Company, Tyneside Pottery Works, Bardon Mill, Hexham NE47 7HU. Telephone: 04984 245

Salt-glazed storage jars and garden pots are made in this pottery, which was established in 1878.

Battlefields

In addition to Flodden (see separate entry, below) the sites of several other of the numerous battles fought in Northumberland may be visited, though none has an interpretation centre.

Halidon Hill (OS 75: NT 972547). About 3 miles north-west of Berwick-upon-Tweed on the north side of A6105. Access via the car park near Camphill. Here the English defeated the Scots in 1333.

Heavenfield (OS 87: NY 936695). 2½ miles east of Chollerford on the north side of B6318. At the lay-by there are a display board and wooden cross. **King Oswald beat Cadwallon in AD 634.**

Hedgeley Moor (OS 81: NU 046197). Near Wooperton, Wooler, on west side of A697. The Yorkists beat the Lancastrians in 1464.

Homildon Hill (OS 75: NT 969295). 1½ miles west of Wooler on the north side of A697. The English beat the Scots in 1402.

Otterburn (Chevy Chase) (OS 80: NY 880940). Reached by footpath from Townhead on the north of the village off A696. The Scots beat the English in 1388.

Chillingham Castle and Wild Cattle, Chillingham, near Wooler. Telephone: 06685 250.

The much altered fourteenth-century castle of the Greys is of four ranges with square corner towers around an internal courtyard. The entrance, on the north, was made grander in the early seventeenth century. In the Norman church two members of the family, Sir Ralph Grey and his wife Elizabeth, are commemorated by a marvellous table tomb of about 1450. Chillingham is chiefly famous for its wild white cattle in the medieval park. Trails to see the shy but aggressive cattle are conducted by a warden. Do not attempt to see them on your own. On the edge of the park is a ruined bastle and, above it, Ross Castle, a hillfort in the care of the National Trust.

Flodden Field, near Branxton (OS 88: NT 8937).

The battle of Flodden Field, at which about nine thousand Scots, including their king, James IV, and five thousand English were slain, took place on 9th September 1513. James had ventured south of the border to avenge the death of his Warden of the Eastern March and had had considerable success, demolishing a number of English castles before his defeat at Flodden. The site of the battle is on Branxton Hill, to the west of the A697, where there is an inscription on an early twentieth-century stone cross commemorating the event. It reads: 'Flodden 1513. To the

CHAPTER 9

Left: *A bull from the herd of wild white cattle at Chillingham.*
Right: *The stone cross commemorating the battle of Flodden.*

brave of both nations.' The battle has captured the popular imagination, partly because of its powerful treatment in Sir Walter Scott's *Marmion* and in the haunting Scottish lament 'The Flowers of the Forest'.

Heatherslaw Corn Mill, Heatherslaw, Cornhill-on-Tweed TD12 4TJ. Telephone: 089082 338.

Heatherslaw Mill is a restored and working water-driven corn mill which is open to the public. There has been milling at this site on the river Till since the thirteenth century. The millstone grinds flour daily, water level permitting, and there is a bakery using the mill's flour and a tea room in the granary. There are displays and exhibitions.

Redesdale Sheep Dairy, Soppit Farm, Elsdon NE19 1AF. Telephone: 0830 20276 or 20506.

At a dairy which has been making cheese from the milk of ewes and cows since 1985 a video shows how the cheese is made. Visitors can watch the sheep being milked each afternoon from Easter to 1st September. Attractions include farm animals, a farm shop and a tea room with home baking.

Twizel Bridge, Tillmouth.

This spectacular single-span bridge over the river Till close to its junction with the river Tweed is thought to date from the fifteenth century. It has now been superseded by a wider modern road bridge.

Above the glen, on the north side of the river, on the site of a fortification which was demolished by James VI, are the remains of Twizel Castle, which was commenced about 1770 but never completed though more portions were added later. Earthworks extend to the north.

Newcastle upon Tyne

The city of Newcastle is spread over a series of hills and valleys on the north bank of the river Tyne. Its situation derives from its being the lowest bridgeable point on the Tyne. The site was chosen by the Romans for a river crossing. They built a bridge, *Pons Aelius*, at a point roughly equating with that of the present-day Swing Bridge, and a fort, part of Hadrian's Wall, to guard it.

Bridges have been crucial to the development of the city. They occasioned the building of structures for their protection, beginning with the Roman fort and continuing with the Norman New Castle. Once a bridge was in position, Newcastle became, and has remained, a natural service centre. That there were a number of tributaries joining the river Tyne at Newcastle was an added advantage to its establishment and growth, since running water is so important for domestic and industrial purposes. The strongest disincentive to development has been the wider geographical position of the city. In earlier times Newcastle was in a frontier zone, first between Romans and Britons, then between English and Scots. The city walls of the late thirteenth century reflect this long-lasting frontier position for, from the decline of the kingdom of Northumbria in the middle Anglo-Saxon period, the area and its main urban settlement have been a long distance from the centre of power to the south.

The good fortune of the presence in quantity in the area surrounding Newcastle of a natural resource, coal, has been the other factor vital to the growth and achievement of the city. The export of coal and of products of coal-dependent processes — the goods frequently made on Tyneside for convenience — has contributed greatly to Newcastle's success. The need to transport coal and other minerals to points of embarkation on the Tyne was responsible for the early use of horse-drawn trucks on wagonways, precursors of railways developed by the Stephensons.

The history of Newcastle, its dependence on trade and industry, is evident in its surviving buildings: the quays, chares and market places, the warehouses and factories, the stately public buildings and thoroughfares, and some handsome private houses. Nonetheless, because so much has changed in recent years, the best place to start a tour of the city and to get a sense of what Tyneside has been all about, is at the Museum of Science and Engineering (see chapter 8) in Blandford Square, where there is large representation of Tyneside in 1929. The immediate impression is of a crowded industrial landscape, criss-crossed by railways, of which the main artery is the river Tyne.

From the museum, it is suggested that the visitor goes to the Quayside, beginning his tour at the Swing Bridge. The present bridge, not as long as its Roman and medieval precursors since the Quayside extended outwards from the riverbank, was built by Lord Armstrong, inventor, manufacturer and major benefactor of the city. His works, with associated workers' housing, was a few miles upstream at Elswick. Walking westwards along the Quay, under Robert Stephenson's High Level rail and road bridge of 1846-9, the visitor will discover the oldest medieval merchant's house remaining on the Quayside. Though heavily restored, it gives an impression of the sort of private houses that must have been a feature of this area at the time.

Back from the Quay, in the Close, is a timber-framed pub, the Cooperage. Along this road, and others in the Quayside-Sandhill area, can be seen various chares and precipitous stairs leading up from the riverside. The steeply inclined area between the Close and Sandhill and the castle became an impoverished ramshackle 'shanty town', while the more salubrious quarters grew up along the bank of the river and its tributaries, and in the 'high town' above. In the Close are several late medieval houses, among them Bessie Surtees' House, now a regional office of English Heritage. From here Bessie, a merchant's daughter, eloped to what was then a humble marriage to the future Lord Eldon, Chancellor of England. The building opposite is the Guildhall, open at one end because it was formerly used as a fish market; on the first floor is a splendid suite of seventeenth-century rooms.

Nearby is the point where the Lort Burn joins the Tyne. From the Sandhill winds the Side, the main medieval route up the hill to St Nicholas's cathedral; it climbs close by the castle and the much later Moot Hall of 1810-12. Continuing east along the riverside, the visitor passes under the 1928 Tyne Bridge; in one of the massive piers is a passenger lift to the road deck.

On the stretch of the Quayside beyond are Victorian commercial buildings, many of them former shipping offices now refurbished for alternative uses, and several narrow chares following the medieval street pattern. On Sundays a lively market is held on the waterfront. On a hill above, approached by steps via King Street and Queen Street, is the elegant

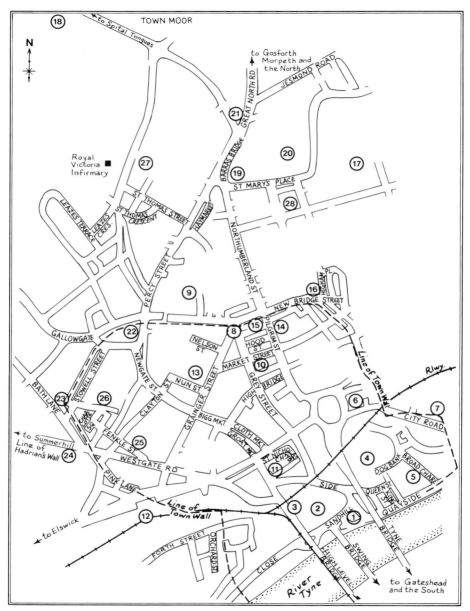

Newcastle upon Tyne. Key: 1 Guildhall, 2 Moot Hall, 3 Castle Keep, 4 All Saints' church, 5 Trinity House, 6 John George Joicey Museum, 7 Sallyport Tower, 8 Grey's Monument, 9 Eldon Square, 10 Theatre Royal, 11 St Nicholas's cathedral, 12 Central station, 13 Grainger Market, 14 Odeon cinema, 15 Tyneside cinema, 16 Laing Art Gallery, 17 Polytechnic, 18 Framlington Place, 19 St Thomas's church, 20 Civic Centre, 21 Hancock Museum, 22 St Andrew's church, 23 Heber Tower, 24 Tyne Theatre, 25 Assembly Rooms, 26 Blackfriars, 27 Museum of Antiquities, 28 City Hall.

eighteenth-century All Saints' church, now home of the educational charity Town Teacher (telephone 091 2616993). Before turning left up Broad Chare, the visitor passes the pedimented eighteenth-century Custom House refaced in the 1830s by the architect Sydney Smirke. The charming complex of Trinity House leads off Broad Chare; it houses the Trinity Maritime Centre (see chapter 8). Though the buildings are mainly eighteenth-century, Trinity House has occupied the site since 1505.

Above Broad Chare, in the City Road is the seventeenth-century brick Holy Jesus Hospital, now the John George Joicey Museum (see chapter 8). On a hill across the valley of the Pandon Burn is a stretch of city wall and the Sallyport Tower, a postern gate. Beyond is the Keelmen's Hospital, an institution which housed the Keelmen and their dependants. Keelmen carried coal in their distinctive boats, keels, to the collier brigs located at the mouth

of the river. It was impossible for the brigs to venture up the river to Newcastle because their draught was too great to be accommodated by the shallow, tidal Tyne before it was dredged in the nineteenth century.

The eastern Quayside area extending to the mouth of the Ouse Burn was formerly the site of considerable commercial and industrial activity. Refurbishment of this part of the city has begun with the building of new law courts and much more is planned. An obelisk marks the spot where John Wesley first preached in Newcastle in 1742. The eighteenth-century St Ann's church can be seen in its bosky hillside location overlooking the Tyne and the Ouse Burn. On the skyline beyond is the much admired early post-modernist exercise in 'community' architecture, the colourful Byker Wall designed by Ralph Erskine.

The focal point of the city now, as it has been since the 1830s, is the monument at the top of Grey Street to the creator of the Reform

Left: The Cooperage, in the Close, Newcastle upon Tyne, with a chare to the right.
Right: St Nicholas's cathedral, Newcastle upon Tyne, with the castle's Black Gate to the right.

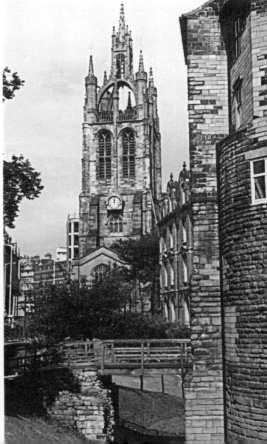

Bill, Earl Grey. On Saturdays it is possible to climb its steep stairs and obtain a splendid bird's eye view of Tyneside, and more especially of the network of streets forming the early nineteenth-century planned town. This was a product of the entrepreneurial skills of the builder Richard Grainger, town clerk John Clayton and architects John Dobson and Thomas Oliver. Not all of their grandiose schemes were built, and of those that were some have been pulled down, altered or are not well maintained.

A *cause célèbre* was the demolition in the 1960s of most of Dobson's Eldon Square to make way for the glossy shopping centre of the same name. Nonetheless, the view of the curve of Grey Street is one of the best sights in Newcastle. Grey Street embraces many fine classical sandstone buildings, including the refurbished Theatre Royal and Lloyds Bank, the latter on the site of the Greyfriars, subsequently used for a sixteenth-century mansion and huge garden, a town house of the Blacketts called Anderson Place.

It is worth exploring the side streets off Grey Street, such as Hood Street, Market Street and High Bridge. The last was built over the course

All Saints' church, Newcastle upon Tyne.

of the Lort Burn, which became such a health risk that it was covered over in the nineteenth century. The late Victorian tiled Central Arcade is modestly notable too. High Bridge leads into the Bigg Market and the associated Groat Market and Cloth Market, all near to the cathedral, the centre of the medieval city. In St Nicholas's Churchyard is the site of the workshop of the engraver Thomas Bewick.

Of other classical streets radiating from Grey's Monument, Grainger Street leads nobly towards Dobson's Central Station. On its north side are Nelson and Nun Streets, flanking the splendid covered Grainger Market, designed by Dobson in 1835. The north entrance to the market is from Clayton Street, which extends across Newgate Street southwestwards to become West Clayton Street after crossing Westgate Road. All form part of the ambitious concept, instigated by Grainger, Clayton, Dobson and Oliver, of a uniformly classical town centre.

Parallel with Grey Street is Pilgrim Street. At its top, near the site of the Pilgrim Gate, a north gate out of the walled city, are two fine inter-war cinemas, the Odeon and the smaller Tyneside. Further down, near the modern Swan Roundabout named after the inventor Sir Joseph Swan, who developed his electric lamps on Tyneside, is the old Liberal Club, a beautiful brick town house of Alderman Fenwick, built about 1700 and newly restored. The road east from the top of Pilgrim Street is New Bridge Street; at Number 49 John Dobson built himself a discreetly elegant neo-classical house. Opposite is Dobson's Gothic Lying-in Hospital of 1826. On the corner of New Bridge Street and Higham Place is the Edwardian Laing Art Gallery.

East and north of Northumberland Street, into an area occupied by the many buildings of the Polytechnic, and extending as far as Jesmond Road — the 'border' with Jesmond — and beyond later university buildings to leafy pedestrian Framlington Place, is the surviving part of a sequence of nineteenth-century classical squares and streets. These represent a natural extension of the urban style of Grainger and his colleagues.

At the top of Northumberland Street is a Gothic Dobson group of the sombre St Thomas's church and the gabled row of St Mary's Place. Beyond them to the north is the Scandinavian-style Civic Centre of 1968. The Hancock Museum (see chapter 8), on a bluff overlooking the site of the former Barras Bridge, though built in 1878, is a classical building which is reminiscent of the style of Dobson. Barras Bridge crossed the Pandon Burn before the water was concealed underground.

North-west of the Haymarket, which leads from the location of the old Barras Bridge, is

Leazes Terrace, Newcastle upon Tyne.

the delightful St Thomas's area. This comprises a crescent and associated streets of houses and mews in simple classical style; beneath runs the Lort Burn. On their northern edge, facing Leazes Park, is Leazes Crescent by Thomas Oliver. Extending into what was once open Moor, forming an inside-out square, is the massively spectacular Leazes Terrace, designed by Oliver in 1829. At that time it was envisaged that the Leazes enclave should be linked more closely to the town centre scheme by means of an elegant sweep of new road, but this was never built.

Down the hill from the Leazes area, on the west side of the city centre, some impressive stretches of the medieval city wall remain. This can be followed from Gallowgate, first along the north side of the graveyard of St Andrew's church, next along the cobbled and narrow medieval intramural road behind Stowell Street in the lively Chinese quarter, and then, turning south from the wall's north-western corner, beside Bath Lane. A series of towers and a postern, as well as the wall itself, are well preserved. Just outside it, by Heber Tower, is the House of Recovery, a fever hospital built in 1804 and now restored to be the headquarters of the North of England Museums Service.

The area around Bath Lane and the Westgate Road is also being rejuvenated. The Tyne Theatre has re-opened after a lavish restoration and many small specialist shops are opening in refurbished premises. There are an arts centre and a dance studio. The National Trust Information Centre is at 73 Westgate Road. Nearby in Fenkle Street are the elegant eighteenth-century Assembly Rooms. The west end of Fenkle Street leads to the once smart Charlotte Square, now being refurbished. Under a modern arch at its north corner is an alleyway leading to the buildings of the medieval Blackfriars (Dominicans). Here are a craft and tourist information centre, displays on both Newcastle's history and that of this site, an excavation of most of the friary church consolidated for visitors to see, and a restaurant.

South of the Westgate Road, the city wall followed a line from the Pink Tower along Pink Lane and thence its line traversed land later covered by the Central Station. The wall then continued from the Neville Tower, parallel with Orchard Street, where a considerable upstanding length may again be seen, and east of the Forth Banks area, where Stephenson's works were situated, to the Close Gate and, finally, to the Riverside Tower.

Newcastle has some fascinating suburbs. On its west, off Westgate Road and Hill is the secluded Summerhill area. Terraces and a square have long gardens and a pleasant aspect facing south across the Tyne valley. In Greenfield Place Robert Stephenson lived for a time.

At the top of the hill is the broodingly handsome pinnacled church of St Matthew. Beyond are large Victorian town houses, originally built in attractive surroundings on high ground overlooking the river. On the lower levels is what remains of the Armstrong company town of Elswick.

To the north of Newcastle is the vast expanse of the Town Moor. Though now a little encroached upon by roads and some buildings, it is still rural in character and essentially as it was intended to be, a grazing and recreation area. In June the celebrated town fair, the Hoppings, is held there. Horse races were once held there too but they were transferred to Gosforth Park in 1882. On the south-western edge of the Moor is Spital Tongues, formerly the site of an isolation hospital and later of a mining community; it is now visually dominated by blocks of students' accommodation, Castle Leazes, dwarfing Fenham Barracks. In Claremont Road is a survivor of the many windmills that once surrounded the city. It was built of clapboard, with five sails, in 1782 to the design of the famous engineer John Smeaton. It was in use for only twenty years, subsequently served as a golf clubhouse and has now been restored, albeit without its sails.

East of the city is the essentially nineteenth-century suburb of Jesmond. The cemetery in Jesmond Road is a lugubrious manifestation of the Victorian way of death; its entrance gates were designed by Dobson in 1839. Jesmond and the neighbouring community of Heaton are linked by the wooded, cavernous gorge of the Ouse Burn, bordered at intervals by suitably Gothic villas, though in some places there are traces of houses of earlier periods.

The series of parks leading into one another on a north-south axis is a popular place for walks. Much of this picturesque area was acquired by Lord Armstrong at various stages and donated to the city for public use in 1883. At the southern end is Heaton Park, embellished with fallen classical masonry; in its north-eastern corner are the ruins of a tower house, known as King John's Palace. There is also a splendid newly restored pavilion in Heaton Park. Beyond is Jesmond Vale Lane, which forms the boundary with Armstrong Park. The bucolic sweep of Armstrong Park is spanned by a small bridge to allow cattle to cross to the Ouse Burn, a characteristically philanthropic gesture by Lord Armstrong.

A main road to the coast, at this point named Benton Bank, separates Armstrong Park and Jesmond Dene; alongside it is the delicate metal Armstrong Bridge, upon which an art and craft show is held on Sundays. To its north, in Jesmond Dene, is the popular Pets' Corner. Further north, on the opposite side of the Ouse Burn, is the ruined Banqueting Hall, designed by Dobson. Beyond, along the top near Jesmond Dene Road, is a group of gaunt Victorian houses, residences of successful local businessmen; among them are Jesmond Dene House and Jesmond Dene Towers. Below is a waterfall and the old mill. The northernmost entrance to the Dene is at Castle Farm Bridge, near the eighteenth-century Castle Farm.

There is a lot to see in Newcastle. One of the best ways to obtain an impression of the variety of the city and its environs is to make a round trip on the Metro, travelling in an easterly direction to the coast and returning through the northern suburbs.

The five bridges over the Tyne at Newcastle.

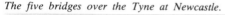

Derelict industrial landscape, Allendale Common.

11
Towns and villages

ALLENDALE TOWN

A former market town occupying a prominent position in the valley of the East Allen river, Allendale was a centre of lead mining which reached its zenith in the eighteenth and nineteenth centries. There is a large bonfire celebration, of ancient derivation, at Allendale Town on New Year's Eve. The town is the geophysical centre of Great Britain, according to a sundial in the Market Place. St Cuthbert's parish church overlooks the pretty riverside site on the outskirts of the town which, in the late summer, is the location of the annual Allendale Show.

ALLENHEADS

An estate village of Allenheads Park at the head of the East Allen valley, this was formerly a busy place, a centre of industrial activity in Allendale of which the scars still remain. At Allenheads was the largest silver-lead mine in the world until its closure in 1896. The village was in decline until 1986 but, after a newspaper article highlighted its distress, efforts, spearheaded by the Development Commission, have been made to set the village on its feet. These include the conversion of buildings for use as a heritage centre and as holiday accommodation; the pleasant village inn has been revamped. The surrounding moors, which show much evidence of lead mining in former times, are spectacular walking and riding country, with skiing in winter.

ALNHAM

The grassy mound of the early medieval castle dominates this village in its remote and scenic location. Alongside the small thirteenth-century church is a vicar's pele. Among earthworks in the area are three late prehistoric settlements on Castlehill and High Knowes (see chapter 3).

ALNMOUTH

The picturesque village is a familiar site to travellers on the main railway line to and from Edinburgh, though the station is about a mile inland. Alnmouth is now mainly a holiday village, a centre for boating and golf. Its origins are at least as old as the eighth century, when the village was a focus for early Christian religious activity. During the medieval period it became an important coastal port. The main export in the eighteenth century was corn. The town was described by John Wesley as 'famous for all kinds of wickedness'. Fine beaches extend from the village. There are good walks north to the fishing village of Boulmer, reputedly a smugglers' haunt, and south past Birling Carrs to Warkworth.

ALNWICK

Early closing Wednesday; market day Saturday.

The headquarters of the Percy dynasty and former county town, Alnwick has a border air. The Percy family seat, Alnwick Castle, and its extensive grounds, Hulne Park, dominate the market town. Straight-tailed lions, the Percy badge, surmount the Lion Bridge over the river Aln of 1773 by John Adam at the town's north end and an elegant column monument — erected by tenants — at its south. The castle (see chapter 6), dating from the eleventh century, was acquired by the Percys in 1309. It was extensively remodelled in the Gothic style by Salvin in the nineteenth century; the Victorian Italianate interior decoration is complemented by paintings by Canaletto, Titian and Van Dyck and a renowned collection of Meissen porcelain. In Hulne Park, part of which was designed by the Northumbrian Lancelot 'Capability' Brown, are remains of the early Carmelite monastery of Hulne Priory, dating from 1240 (see chapter 5), and Brislee Tower, a gazebo thought to have been designed by Robert Adam.

Alnwick is a good place to explore on foot. Its streets bear much evidence of its status as an estate town. The Hotspur Gate, forming part of the fifteenth-century town fortifications, gives access from Bondgate Without to Bondgate Within and the Market Place. There is much fine architecture, notably in Bailiffgate, a noble street leading to the castle from the fifteenth-century St Michael's church, which was much altered in the nineteenth century by the north-eastern architect Dobson, Salvin and others. Among the buildings flanking the Market Place are the elegant Town Hall of 1771 and the White Swan Inn, which houses the first-class lounge from the *Olympic*, a sister ship of the ill-fated *Titanic*. Alnwick Fair, which derives from a 1297 market fair, takes place for a week in June or July.

AMBLE

Amble is a somewhat dour small port below Warkworth at the mouth of the river Coquet. Its major livelihood was the export of coal and as that trade dwindled the town went into decline. However, it has now been revived with the construction of a marina on the site of the former staithes along the estuary. The marina has twice won European environmental awards and the harbour is now home to a fleet of fishing cobles, whose catch can be sampled locally. Druridge Bay Country Park is being created on reclaimed mining land to the south. Offshore is Coquet Island (see chapter 2).

ASHINGTON

A huge mining conurbation flanking the river Wansbeck, Ashington is perceived by its natives to be a village. Although the place is now in deep decline, it looks quite prosperous. There are rows of terraced houses built in the late nineteenth century and early to mid twentieth century. The village is renowned for the cultivation of superlative footballers and leeks. A park along the riverbanks provides

Northumberland Hall (1826) in the Market Place, Alnwick.

Belford Hall across the park.

recreational facilities. In the late Saxon church at nearby Woodhorn is a museum, with temporary exhibitions and other cultural activities (see chapter 5). The Woodhorn Colliery Museum, in preparation, is to display the history of Northumberland coal mining.

BAMBURGH

An unspectacular village around a triangular green is visually closed to the east by the dominating presence of the castle (see chapter 6) at the end of the main street. Grace Darling, saviour of the survivors from the Longstone wreck, is buried here. She is commemorated by a memorial outside St Aidan's church and in a small museum (see chapter 8). Unfortunate inter-war villas stand on the high ground, but there is a splendid beach. There are good walks north along the coast to Budle Bay, a focus of bird life, and Waren Mill, and south to Seahouses.

BEDLINGTON

Some of its former eminence as capital of the area known as Bedlingtonshire is still evident in the plan and architecture of Bedlington, once in the County Palatine of Durham, later a mining village. In the main street, called Front Street, are good-looking houses, the market cross and the much altered late Norman church. At Bedlington the iron rails for the first public railway, the Stockton to Darlington, were made, and the place is home of the Bedlington terrier.

BELFORD
Early closing Thursday.

Belford is an interesting small town set amidst fertile arable land on the main road north. It is now somewhat isolated, having been avoided by the railway and separated by a bypass from its main link with the outside world, the A1. At the top of the broad street, which still retains some old shop fronts, is a former coaching inn, the Blue Bell; behind are a noble church, of Norman origin and restored by Dobson, and churchyard on a knoll. After years of neglect, the Palladian-style Belford Hall, designed by James Paine, has been elegantly restored to form a number of residential units. Unfortunately unsightly encroachment on to its park has taken place.

BELLINGHAM
Market day Monday.

A former centre of industrial activity — there was a large ironworks — this market village occupies an important position in the North Tyne valley. In the past the village was the natural object of raids from Scotland. The Anglican church is of thirteenth-century origin. The Roman Catholic church of 1839 is by Bonomi. Bellingham now functions as a gateway and service point for visitors to the attractions of Kielder Forest and Water, as well as for the local farming community. For both roles, the many pubs are a useful resource. The railway, which passed through the village and on up the valley to Kielder, has

Blanchland: the view from County Durham at the south end of the bridge across the river Derwent.

gone. Bellingham is the starting point of a walk to Hareshaw Linn waterfall (see chapter 2).

BERWICK-UPON-TWEED
Early closing Thursday; market days Wednesdays and Saturdays.

Its position on the north side of the Tweed estuary indicates that the nationality of the town has been the subject of dispute through history. Though now Northumbrian, Berwick's long status as a free town gives it an air of independence. The links with the rest of Northumberland are three bridges: the earliest dates from 1610-34, but the most famous is the Royal Border Bridge of 1847 by Robert Stephenson, which carries the railway.

The dominating features of Berwick, and the most renowned, are its fortifications, even though the castle was obliterated by the railway. The extensive Italianate Elizabethan fortress defences are dispersed in a formal pattern of bastions snaking round the headland, encompassing the medieval town. Of the many fine classical buildings within, the most spectacular are the mid seventeenth-century Holy Trinity church on Wallace Green, which contains the earliest reredos by Lutyens, and the Barracks, maybe to the design of John Vanbrugh, dating to 1719.

Among the many interesting eighteenth-century buildings in the town are the Governor's Palace on Palace Green and the Town Hall dominating Marygate; others of note are situated in Ravensdowne and Palace Street East. It is well worth walking right round the town, following the line of the walls. Good views are obtained from Halidon Hill, northwest of Berwick, which in 1333 was the site of a Scottish victory. The swans on the river, and the salmon in it, are famed.

BLANCHLAND
A picture-postcard place in the south-west of the county, Blanchland abuts former areas of lead mining, to which most of its present form relates. Though much of the village was planned and built by trustees of the Crewe estate in the eighteenth century to accommodate mine-workers, its nucleus is the abbey founded in 1165. At the top of the square is a fifteenth-century gatehouse; the other end leads off to a bridge over the river Derwent.

BLYTH
Once a major north-east coast port and shipbuilding and industrial centre, the town is now sadly down at heel. Coal was the main export. Blyth essentially dates from the eighteenth century, though it is claimed that a railway was laid here in the early seventeenth century for the transport of coal to the riverside. The town's coal staithes have been demolished and its fishing harbour is only a

shadow of its former self but there is still a strong air of grit and salt about the place. It has a lighthouse of 1788 in the centre of the town and two piers where they ought to be, though the long northern one is now closed to pedestrians. The dour suburb of North Blyth can still be reached by a beguiling little passenger ferry. A long beach, much patronised by the locals, extends south to Seaton Sluice.

BYWELL

This idyllic hamlet on the north side of the river Tyne has two churches (see chapter 5): St Andrew's, one of the clutch of Anglo-Saxon churches in the Tyne valley; and St Peter's, probably eleventh-century in origin, although much of the fabric is of the thirteenth century. Across a field, amongst luxuriant vegetation, is the romantic ruin of Bywell Castle, a fifteenth-century fortified gatehouse turned into a house. Bywell Hall is a classical house, designed by James Paine in the eighteenth century for the Fenwick family, and altered by Dobson in 1817. Its surrounding parkland is lush, and the estate and its buildings, which extend up the hill and over a fine river bridge to Stocksfield, are in fine fettle.

Bywell was regarded in the sixteenth century as a town. Its decline, beginning in the eighteenth century, may be attributable to the dwindling of its fishing and ironworking industries. Present appearances very much reflect the creation of a parkland landscape around the hall. The area is the subject of detailed survey by Durham University's Department of Archaeology.

CAMBO

The immaculate model village of about 1740 of the Wallington estate (see chapter 7) is centred on a medieval tower house, now the post office. The landscape architect 'Capability' Brown, who was brought up at nearby Kirkharle, went to school here. The village is now largely owned by the National Trust.

CORBRIDGE

Early closing Thursday.

A town with a rather turbulent history that now has a cosy, even chichi, aspect, Corbridge was at first the furthest point north on Dere Street, the Roman road from York. The excavated Roman fort and later supply base and the accompanying site museum (see chapters 4 and 8) are located across fields to the west of the present town, whose nucleus is the church, with an Anglo-Saxon tower. Alongside it is the vicar's pele of about 1300. The base of the tower of the church is thought to pre-date the death in the town of Ethelred, king of Northumbria, in AD 796. Its upper portion is later, probably eleventh-century. In the Market Place is an 1814 cast iron cross. The Angel Inn, located in the wide Main Street, and the Wheatsheaf Inn, formerly a

Bywell Castle, just visible centre right, with part of the empty town site in the foreground.

farmhouse, situated at the head of Watling Street, are both seventeenth-century buildings and as such are relatively early survivals of their kind in Northumberland. Another very wide thoroughfare is Hill Street, flanked by pleasant buildings. A short steep scarp leads down to the river and bridge of 1674.

CRASTER

This estate fishing village of Craster Tower, a tunnel-vaulted building dating from the fifteenth century, added to in 1769, is separated from the tower by an outcrop of the Whin Sill. Craster kippers are deservedly renowned; there is still a smoke-house. The village is the starting point for a coastal walk to Dunstanburgh Castle (see chapter 6), which dominates the skyline to the north.

CULLERCOATS

Until it lost trade to Blyth up the coast in the eighteenth century, Cullercoats exported coal and salt. It was once a picturesque and

Corbridge: the cast iron cross in the Market Place.

fiercely independent fishing village famous for its formidable fishwives, who, in their distinctive pintucked skirts, travelled the neighbourhood selling fish. The village also became a haunt of artists, including the American Winslow Homer, who in 1881-2 resided near the 1879 clifftop Watch House.

Post-war modernisation has removed much of the distinctiveness of Cullercoats, but what remains includes Cliff House of 1774, the Rocket former Life Brigade House of 1867, now a garage, a few much altered single-storey fishermen's cottages, and the Seamen's Mission. Towards Tynemouth, the dramatic Victorian church (chapter 5) is close to some splendid Edwardian arts and crafts villas. The protected sandy cove of Cullercoats still has charm; in one corner is the Edwardian Dove Marine Laboratory, part of the University of Newcastle upon Tyne.

ELSDON

The village was formerly the capital of Redesdale. Situated beside the Elsdon Burn, it possesses a large green and is overlooked by the motte and bailey of an early Norman castle (see chapter 6). At the top of the green is a fourteenth-century vicar's pele; to the south and on the green are the church, of similar date, and a stone-walled animal pound. The moorland landscape hereabouts is drear or spectacular, depending on your point of view.

ETAL

The eighteenth-century Etal Manor is the home of the Joicey family; its chapel is by Butterfield. The garden is renowned for its rhododendrons. Between the manor and the fourteenth-century castle (see chapter 6) extends the 'toy-town' street of the pretty grey and white estate village. The houses date from the eighteenth to twentieth centuries; some, including the pub, are thatched. The ruined castle, on a promontory overlooking the river Till, is being repaired. A narrow road alongside it leads down to an old ford where there was, until it was swept away in floods in the sixteenth century, a bridge. There is, however, still a suspension footbridge. A footpath leads to Twizel.

FORD

The baronial-style four-cornered Ford Castle is situated on a hill above an ancient crossing of the river Till and dates originally from the fourteenth century. In 1513 the castle was the headquarters of James IV before he moved on to Flodden Field (see chapter 9). The castle received Gothick alterations in the eighteenth century when it was acquired by the Delaval family. Through the marriage of a Delaval daughter to a Marquis of Waterford the property was transferred into the Water-

Craster harbour.

ford family, in whose care it remained until it was purchased by the Joiceys (see Etal). A Waterford widow was responsible for the nineteenth-century remodelling of the castle and the rebuilding of the village for the benefit of the tenants. The resulting model village is a mass of charming detail. Its showpiece is the former school, now known as the Lady Waterford Gallery (see chapter 8), in which are biblical scenes painted by Lady Waterford.

Between the church and the castle, in what is known as the Glebe Field, is the portion of a pele tower, probably early sixteenth-century, which is all that remains after its partial demolition by Lady Waterford, who thought the pele spoilt her view from the castle.

HARBOTTLE

This pleasant village on the river Coquet was formerly capital of the Middle March. There are remains of the twelfth-century castle, built for Henry II, on a mound, the site of an earlier fortification. The other Harbottle Castle, also known as Castle House, is an 1829 shooting box designed by Dobson, now subdivided into smaller units. The village is a good base for exploring the northern portion of the Northumberland National Park; the Park has an information centre in Harbottle.

HARTBURN

This hilltop village lies near the confluence of the river Wansbeck and a tributary. At the waterside is an eighteenth-century tower built by the vicar of Hartburn, a Dr Sharpe, and his congregation. In the thirteenth-century church is a memorial to the celebrated historian of Northumberland, John Hodgson.

HEXHAM

Early closing Thursday; market day Tuesday.

Hexham is a hill town that extends down to the cattle and sheep markets, the railway station and the south bank of the river Tyne. It services a large area of south-western Northumberland. At its heart are the abbey (see also chapter 5), built about AD 675-80 at the direction of St Wilfrid, and the Market Place next to it. The abbey, like many buildings in Hexham, contains Roman stones. The crypt is largely original, though the remainder of the abbey was much altered after it was adopted in 1113 by the Augustinian canons as a priory church and again in the Victorian and Edwardian periods. There are two medieval towers in the town: the fourteenth-century Manor Office housing the Middle March Centre (see chapter 8), in which the history of the Border is presented, and a tourist information centre; and the Moot Hall, dating from the fourteenth or early fifteenth century. Among other early buildings is the Priory Gate of about 1160. There is a seventeenth-century Grammar School. There is an attractive public park near

Vicar's pele, Elsdon.

the abbey and on the water meadows is Tyne Green Riverside Country Park. The racecourse is some distance south-west of the town.

HOLYSTONE

This is a tiny picturesque village in the Coquet valley. A short walk up the stream that runs through the pub grounds leads to the atmospheric Lady Well, where St Paulinus is alleged to have carried out as many as three thousand baptisms on one day in Easter Week, AD 627; the well, which flanks the Roman road linking Redesdale and the Northumbrian coast, is now in the ownership of the National Trust. An Augustinian nunnery occupied the site of the tiny nineteenth-century church. There is a pele tower in the grounds of Holystone Grange which can be clearly seen from the road.

INGRAM

This is a hamlet in the idyllic Ingram valley. A road leads up the wide valley bottom, offering the motorist an opportunity to experience some of the best landscape of upland Northumberland. It is an ideal spot for picnics by the river Breamish. More energetic visitors

can find many good walks emanating from the valley. There is a National Park information centre close to the village. Archaeological sites abound in the hills around (see chapter 3).

KIRKNEWTON

A village close to the meeting point of the College Burn and the river Glen, Kirknewton is dominated by the iron age hillfort of Yeavering Bell to the south (see chapter 3). In the early medieval church is a sculpture of the Magi in kilts, thought to be of twelfth-century date.

KIRKWHELPINGTON

This pretty village at the moor edge on a promontory overlooking a secluded portion of the Wansbeck valley is bypassed by the A696 Newcastle to Jedburgh road. St Bartholomew's church was founded in Norman times. A charming garden tumbles down to a stately small bridge over the Wansbeck; downstream is a mill. The older architecture indicates that in the nineteenth century Kirkwhelpington was a mining village. For nine years from 1823 it was the home of the Northumbrian historian John Hodgson (see also Hartburn). At nearby Kirkharle the landscape architect Lancelot 'Capability' Brown was born in 1715.

LINDISFARNE

Lindisfarne, also known as Holy Island, is accessible from the mainland only when the tide is low. It is one of the earliest major Christian sites in England. The missionary St Aidan landed here in AD 635, having come from Iona at the request of the Northumbrian king, Oswald. Aidan founded a see and a monastery, subsequently obliterated by the Danes; in AD 875 the Bishop of Durham refounded a monastery on the island, establishing links between the bishopric of Durham and Lindisfarne.

The main sites on the island are the Norman priory and accompanying museum (see chapters 5 and 8) and, high on a rocky outcrop of the Whin Sill, the sixteenth-century castle, rebuilt to the design of Edwin Lutyens early in the twentieth century for the founder of *Country Life* magazine, Edward Hudson (see chapter 7).

Among other buildings and monuments of particular interest on Lindisfarne are: the fortification work on the headland south of the priory; the alleged cell of St Cuthbert on a tiny 'island' that is cut off at high tide; an impressive limekiln on the shore beneath the castle, and the windswept castle garden designed by Gertrude Jekyll; the restored tide mill on marshes below the medieval harbour high-tide line; the fishermen's huts formed of overturned halves of boats; and a pit-shaft tower at the north-west end of the island in an area known as the Snook.

There is a small village around the priory. It is spoilt by twentieth-century accretions along the shore towards the causeway to the mainland. In winter Lindisfarne is a focus for seabirds, especially on its landward side. Part of Lindisfarne is a National Nature Reserve. There are splendid walks all over the island, which is about 3½ miles (6 km) long, and approximately 1 mile (1.5 km) across at its widest point. From the south end of the island there are views to the beacon obelisks on the mainland shore, which are maintained by Trinity House; they were built in 1860 to guide shipping carrying lime and coal to and from Holy Island.

LOWICK

A somewhat surprising street village, on an east-west axis now, Lowick is situated on the Roman road south from Tweedmouth. About halfway along the north side of the main street is a row of peach-washed 'estate' houses with stone window surrounds, looking distinctly Scottish. Maybe the houses are by the same architect as nearby Barmoor Castle, designed in 1801 by Patterson, a Scot. With several houses of substance, the village is unlike the farm hamlets more usual hereabouts. A back street called Cheviot View overlooks a square. There is a Roman Catholic church as well as a Church of England one and a large chapel. The whole gives an impression of a quarrying and mining village, despite what appear to be a few farms fronting on to the main street.

LOW NEWTON

A small early nineteenth-century fishing village with a pub and shop, grouped round a square, Low Newton is owned by the National Trust. From Low Newton there is a pleasant walk on the sands or dunes past the Newton Pool Reserve bird sanctuary, round Embleton Bay, to Dunstanburgh Castle. On Newton Point, just north-east of the village, cowslips bloom in spring. There is a car park at the

Lindisfarne: limekilns, castle and, in the distance, the Priory and parish church by the village.

Low Newton, looking from the shore across the village square.

approach to the village.

MATFEN

Matfen Hall, a sprawling house built in 1823-32 for Sir Edward Blackett, a member of a prominent Northumbrian family, is now a Cheshire Home. The church is mid Victorian. The cottage gardens are pretty and luxuriant perhaps because a babbling stream runs through the centre of the compact village; the surrounding farmland is on the back doorstep. It appears from the position of the earlier buildings facing the church that the main street was once a back lane until Matfen became the estate village of Matfen Hall. There is an attractive former village school.

MITFORD

A pretty gentrified village, Mitford lies at the confluence of the river Font with the Wansbeck. Of the castle overlooking the Wansbeck valley there has been little to see since the destruction of the fabric by the Scots early in the fourteenth century. Mitford Hall, like Meldon Park a few miles further west, is an example of a Dobson country house in neo-classical style.

MORPETH

Early closing Thursday; market day Wednesday.

A pleasant town on a bend in the river Wansbeck, Morpeth has become reinvigorated since gaining the status of county town when Newcastle became part of Tyne and Wear. The remains of a Norman and later castle overlook what was a medieval planned town, in the centre of which stand the unusual seventeenth-century clock-tower and the nearby Town Hall, which, though much altered, was built in 1714 to the design of John Vanbrugh. The elegant road bridge over the Wansbeck, sited with Telford's approval and designed by Dobson about 1830, replaced the double-arched medieval bridge whose pier and abutments now carry a footbridge of 1869. Both bridges link Castle Green to the 'new' town. Fronting the Green like a toy-town fort is Dobson's spectacular Court House, gate-house to the county jail (1829-81) and now a restaurant with private accommodation in the former prisoners' blocks behind.

In the thirteenth-century Chantry building are the acclaimed Bagpipe Museum (see chapter 8) and a craft centre and tourist information centre. Morpeth is one of the few places in Northumberland where it is still possible to rent river rowing boats. The custom of Riding the Bounds is retained. Among several Morpeth worthies is Admiral Collingwood, who took over command from Nelson at the battle of Trafalgar; his house is in Oldgate. In Cottingwood Lane, one of several attractive streets worthy of exploration, was the King Edward VI Grammar School, the Victorian version having been demolished to make way for a new comprehensive school further up the lane. Off the former cattle market, with an outlook to Carlisle Park on the opposite riverbank, is a secluded post-modernist retirement development.

NEWCASTLE UPON TYNE

See chapter 10.

NORHAM

St Aidan crossed the Tweed here in AD 635 on his way to Lindisfarne from Iona. It became a stronghold of the Prince Bishops of Durham on the frontier with Scotland and the centre of Norhamshire. The early Norman castle of the Palatinate, looked after by English Heritage, is on a hill above (see chapter 6). The fine church dates from 1165 and has a huge churchyard; an earlier church on the site was built in AD 875. A reminder of the more peaceful concerns of this long green village and of others along the banks of the Tweed is the Blessing the Nets ceremony. This takes place at Norham each year, at midnight on 13th February, marking the beginning of the salmon-fishing season.

NORTH SHIELDS

A town traditionally associated with fishing, shipbuilding and the export of coal, sharing these and other concerns with many communities on Tyneside, North Shields is unusual in having been the subject of ambitious plans in the later eighteenth and early nineteenth centuries for the addition of a new town, though many of these never reached fruition. New Quay, from which the only ferry across the Tyne has departed for at least five hundred years, is an example of the elegant buildings that were a part of the concept. Though only a portion of the square was ever built — the Northumberland Arms in 1816 and the Sailors' Home eventually in 1856 — drawings of the original scheme for the square show how superb the whole would have looked: a little Greenwich of the north. Close by is Smith's Dock.

Up-town, most of the gracious Northumberland Square of about 1800 remains. Among isolated terraces of slightly later date is the charming Rosella Place in Albion Road. To its east is the interesting and rather elegant Christ Church, first built as the parish church of Tynemouth in 1658-68, then rebuilt in 1792. Further north still, off Preston Road, is Camp Terrace, middle to late nineteenth-century houses with romantic gardens across the cobbled private road.

Redevelopment is engulfing the heart of the town. Howard Street, which leads from the elegant former Tynemouth Literary and Philosophical Society library of 1806-7, which became the Stag Line offices, to Northumberland Square, possesses a clutch of Dobson buildings, including the quality 'Tudorbethan' Town Hall, and is still largely intact if rather gloomy. Along the line of Stephenson and Norfolk Streets were two roperies. To the east is Dockwray Square, originally built in 1763, with fine river views, but now largely rebuilt in different form with new houses. On the south side is the New High Light of 1808 and close by at the end of Beacon Street is the Old High Beacon of 1727. Below is one of the best sights of Tyneside, the bustling Fish Quay, which encompasses the New Low Light, and the Old Low Beacon in Clifford's Fort. This is the place to watch the boats come in. To look upstream at this still relatively busy stretch of river is to obtain some impression of what old Tyneside must have been like.

OTTERBURN

In sparsely inhabited Redesdale, the village serves tourists and the army from nearby Otterburn Camp as well as the local community. The site of the battle of Otterburn of 1388 is above the existing village, just to the south-west of Otterburn Hall, now a hotel. Otterburn Tower, of various dates, is a coun-

The clock-tower, Morpeth.

try house hotel in pleasant grounds overlooking one side of the short village street; on the other is the Percy Arms. In the water meadows is the mill, which sells tweeds and jerseys.

ROCK

This is a small village in fertile farming country with a Norman church. Rock Hall, which incorporates a pele tower, is now a youth hostel.

ROTHBURY

Early closing Wednesday.

A late Victorian health resort on a hillside by the Coquet, Rothbury has retained its attraction to visitors. King John, an early visitor, granted Rothbury the right to hold a market and it has been a market town ever since. It is a good base from which to explore the Simonside Hills, which rise to 1409 feet (429 metres) on the south, Cragside house and grounds (see chapter 7) on the north-eastern side of the town, and Brinkburn Priory (see chapter 5) a few miles down river. There is a National Park information centre in Rothbury.

SEAHOUSES

Early closing Wednesday.

A jolly fishing village and holiday resort, built in 1889, Seahouses is the harbour for boat excursions to the Farne Islands (see chapter 2). Immediately to the north are St Aidan's Dunes, in the care of the National Trust. South along the beach at Beadnell is a splendid restored eighteenth-century limekiln, also looked after by the Trust. A National Trust information centre and shop is in Main Street, Seahouses.

SEATON SLUICE

The former name of this place was Hartley

Seahouses harbour and limekilns.

Pans, an indication that from the thirteenth century, for five hundred years until the trade dwindled, there was a salt-pan, fired with local coal, at the mouth of the Seaton Burn.

The fascinating harbour of the flamboyant Delavals was first made in about 1628 to facilitate the export of coal from their estate. The sluice was to flush out silting in the harbour. The impressive cut east through rock to the sea was made in the 1760s — a formidable work. The pretty Octagon overlooking the harbour is perhaps by Vanbrugh, the architect of the Delavals' forbidding baroque house nearby, Seaton Delaval Hall (see chapter 7). The industries of the village were similar to those of many places on Tyneside; at various times there was quarrying, brickmaking, glassworking and bottlemaking.

STAMFORDHAM

The eighteenth-century village around a long green with a cross is designated a conservation area. Across the river is the older settlement represented by earthworks, the thirteenth-century church and the vicarage, originally Tudor.

THOCKRINGTON

An isolated hamlet on a small hill projecting from moorland is surrounded by traces of a formerly larger settlement, supposedly deserted as a result of an outbreak of typhoid. Little is now standing apart from the Norman church, with a tunnel-vaulted chancel, and a farm. A splendid obelisk monument in the windswept churchyard is visible from miles around. Several lakes and reservoirs and the scars of old quarrying characterise the surrounding countryside.

Seaton Sluice: the inner harbour with the cut to the sea under the footbridge beyond.

TYNEMOUTH

The old town has the broad, curving main street and property boundaries at right angles to it characteristic of a planned medieval town. The main thoroughfare, along which are some fine eighteenth-century and early nineteenth-century houses, especially by the junction with the north-south roads, is Front Street.

The town at the mouth of the Tyne stops short of the eastern promontory on which are the ruins of the priory and castle (see chapter 5) and the site of an old lighthouse beyond. The priory, a satellite of St Albans Abbey, is Norman; the castle dates from the late thirteenth and fourteenth centuries. On both sides are beaches; the Short Sands are immediately to the north while to the south the beach is protected by a small bay with a harbour. On the headland, south-west of the bay, above the dangerous river entrance, is the watch-house built in 1886 for the Tynemouth Volunteer Life Brigade, which was formed in 1864, the first of its kind. Further up the grassy sward, overlooking the estuary with its formidable Black Middens rocks, is the commanding monument to Admiral Collingwood, flanked by four cannon from his flagship *Royal Sovereign*, on a plinth designed by Dobson.

The large block beyond is Knott Flats, an example of inter-war rehousing. In contrast, in the foreground is Mariners' Point, a housing association's post-modernist retirement flats encompassing the former Oxford Street station. Nearer the centre of the town is Tyne-mouth station, now part of the excellent Metro system and the subject of an ambitious programme of refurbishment and diversification. Set back from the headland but still with glorious views is a community of mid nineteenth-century terraces, evidence of Tyne-mouth's popularity as a resort which increased with the arrival of the railway.

WARK

A small village amid the sylvan beauty of the valley of the North Tyne, Wark occupied a prominent position in the Norman period as a frontier village with a castle. Little of the latter now remains apart from the steep bank upon which it stood. Nowadays, the centre of the village is a small green; among the buildings which surround it is a farmhouse dating from the sixteenth century. South-east of Wark, overlooking the Tyne, is Chipchase Castle, a fourteenth-century tower house, incorporated within a Jacobean building.

WARKWORTH

Known in Saxon times as *Wercewode*, Warkworth is a good-looking town on a river loop, dominated by the hilltop Percy castle featured in Shakespeare's *Henry IV*. The town plan splendidly preserves its medieval shape and details of burgage plots. The main street descends from the castle to the river Coquet, alongside which is the beautiful Norman church. Its Saxon predecessor was given with the rest of the town in AD 738 to the

59

monastery at Lindisfarne by the king of Northumbria. The medieval bridge, unusually, is fortified with a tower. Bridge End House is early eighteenth-century and has a quiet elegance. The cruciform castle is basically Norman and of the thirteenth and fourteenth centuries. After becoming ruinous it was renovated by Salvin in the mid nineteenth century and made habitable and more ostentatiously romantic, in keeping with the Victorian image of the castle.

There is a beautiful riverside walk along the water meadows from below the castle to the Hermitage (cross by ferry; see chapter 5). In summer rowing boats can be hired to travel upstream; it is possible to land on the north bank and climb the wooded incline to visit the medieval Hermitage and its chapel, both in the custody of English Heritage.

WHALTON

Whalton is a handsome estate village with a wide main street. Sir Edwin Lutyens designed the manor house, created from a group of earlier houses at one end of the village street; Gertrude Jekyll advised on the garden design. A bale-fire is lit on 4th July to commemorate an ancient Old Midsummer Eve custom. At Ogle, 2 miles (3 km) to the south, are a tower house of the fourteenth century and a manor

house dated to one or two centuries later.

WHITLEY BAY

The place for a bracing seaside holiday, the resort has traditionally been popular as a holiday destination with Scots, especially Glaswegians. A landmark is the gleaming white Moorish dome of Spanish City, an amusement park whose future is uncertain. The long stretch of Whitley Sands extends to the causeway leading to St Mary's Island (see chapter 2), accessible only when the tide is low.

WOOLER

A market town on a hillside by Wooler Water, Wooler serves the local community of the Cheviot area and the fertile Milfield basin. The town is a good touring base, with a number of inns, and several camping sites on its outskirts. In the summer there is an information centre at the car park in the High Street.

Wooler is on one of the old routes to Scotland frequented by border reivers (rustlers) — cause for disturbance in the past; the drove road for livestock heading south also passed through the town. The mound and some rubble of the Norman castle are visible, but because two fires burnt the town few of its

Warkworth's medieval bridge was defended by a gate-tower on the town side of the river Coquet.

The fertile area around Wooler looking towards Cheviot.

buildings are older than Victorian. The high ground to its west is thickly covered with visible archaeological sites; a similar density to the north and east is invisible.

12
Tourist information centres

Alnwick: The Shambles, Alnwick NE66 1TN. Telephone: 0665 603129.

Amble: Council Sub Offices, Dilston Terrace, Amble NE65 0DT. Telephone: 0665 712313.

Belford: 2/3 Market Place, Belford NE70 7ND. Telephone: 06683 888.

Bellingham: Main Street, Bellingham NE48 2BQ. Telephone: 0660 20616.

Berwick-upon-Tweed: Castlegate Car Park, Berwick-upon-Tweed TD15 1JS. Telephone: 0289 307187.

Corbridge: The Vicar's Pele, Corbridge NE45 5AW. Telephone: 043471 2815.

Haltwhistle: Tynedale District Sub Office, Sycamore Street, Haltwhistle NE49 0AG. Telephone: 0498 20351.

Hexham: Manor Office, Hallgates, Hexham NE46 1XD. Telephone: 0434 605225.

Kielder Forest: Tower Knowe, Falstone, Hexham NE48 1BX. Telephone: 0660 40398.

Morpeth: The Chantry, Bridge Street, Morpeth NE61 1PJ. Telephone: 0670 511323.

Newcastle Airport, Woolsington, Newcastle upon Tyne NE13 8BU. Telephone: 091 2711929.

Newcastle upon Tyne: City Information Service, Central Library, Princess Square, Newcastle upon Tyne NE99 1DX. Telephone: 091 2615367.

Newcastle upon Tyne: Blackfriars Tourist Centre, Monk Street, Newcastle upon Tyne NE1 4XW. Telephone: 091 2610691.

North Shields: Tyne Commission Quay, North Shields Ferry Terminal, North Shields NE29 6EN. Telephone: 091 2579800.

Seahouses: 16 Main Street, Seahouses NE68 7SR. Telephone: 0665 720424.

Whitley Bay: The Promenade, Whitley Bay NE26 1AZ. Telephone: 091 2524494.

Wooler: Car Park, High Street, Wooler NE71 8LD. Telephone: 0668 81602.

The impressively formal entrance to Chillingham Park and Castle.

NORTHUMBERLAND and NEWCASTLE UPON TYNE

* Countryside site (Ch.2)
⊓ Site of archaeological interest (Ch.3)
H Hadrian's Wall site (Ch.4)
+ Church or abbey (Ch.5)
C Castle or fortification (Ch.6)
▲ Historic house or garden (Ch.7)
M Museum (Ch.8)
o Other places to visit (Ch.9)
■ Town or village (Ch.11)

N

Halidon Hill ○   BERWICK-UPON-TWEED
R.Tweed
Norham +C
+ Ancroft
○ Twizel Bridge
⊓ Duddo Stone Circle
Heatherslaw Mill ○ C Etal   ■ Lowick
Flodden Field ○   M Ford
R.Till
HOLY ISLAND
+▲M
Lindisfarne
* Farne Islands
CM Bamburgh
■ Belford
● Seahouses
Kilham Farm ■ * Old Yeavering
Kirknewton ■   ⊓ Roughting Linn
Yeavering Bell ⊓   ⊓ Dod Law
Hethpool Stone Circle ⊓   ○ Homildon Hill   ■ Wooler
⊓ Fredden Hill
Preston Tower C
○ Chillingham Castle   ● Low Newton
Hedgeley Moor *   ⊓+ Old Bewick   C Dunstanburgh Castle
THE CHEVIOT   Dod Hill ⊓   ● Rock   ● Craster
Howick Garden ▲
Greave's Ash ⊓⊓   ⊓ Ingram
⊓ Brough Law   R.Aln   + Hulne Priory
High Knowes ⊓   ■ Alnham   C M ALNWICK
Alnmouth
Chew Green *   C Edlingham Castle
Harbottle ■   Warkworth
⊓⊓ Holystone   Rothbury   C+   * Coquet Island
Bellshiel Law ⊓   ▲ Cragside   Amble
Simonside Forest Walks *   + Brinkburn Priory
Lordenshaws   Druridge Bay
Kielder Castle *   C Elsdon
Bakethin Reservoir   Otterburn ■   O
Redesdale Dairy
KIELDER FOREST   Black Middens Bastle C
Kielder Water   Rothley Crags *   Newminster Abbey +   ASHINGTON   + Woodhorn
Leaplish   Hareshaw Linn *   Hartburn   M R.Wansbeck   MORPETH
Visitor Centre *   Cambo ■   Mitford
R.North Tyne   Kirkwhelpington   + Bolam   BEDLINGTON
Bellingham ■   Wellington Hall ▲   ■ Whalton   R.Blyth   BLYTH
■ Thockrington   ▲ Belsay Hall   * Plessey Woods
■ Wark   Seaton Delaval Hall ▲   ● Seaton Sluice
Black Carts H   Chesters H   * St Mary's Island
Sewingshields Housesteads H H   HM Brunton   ■ Matfen   ■ Stamfordham   Killingworth   WHITLEY BAY
Roman Army Museum M   H Carrawburgh   ○ Heavenfield   Heddon-on-the-Wall   M   Cullercoats +
Once Brewed HM   Planetrees   TYNEMOUTH +
Bardon Mill ○   Warden +   R.Tyne   C Aydon Castle   + Welton   + Denton Hall   M+ NORTH SHIELDS
HM Chesterholm   South Tyne R   Corbridge C   Wylam H   HM   H Wallsend
HADRIAN'S WALL   Bellister Castle C   * Allenbanks   Bywell   C+ Prudhoe Castle   Benwell H
C Langley Castle   + HEXHAM   ■ Mickley   Ovingham   NEWCASTLE UPON TYNE
Tyne Riverside Country Park

■ Allendale Town

* Derwent Reservoir
R.Allen   ■ Blanchland

■ Allenheads

0   10   20   30 Kms.
0   5   10   15   20 Miles

Index